LONG AND SHORT:
Confessions of a Portfolio Manager

LONG AND SHORT:
Confessions of a Portfolio Manager

Stock Market Wisdom for Investors

Lawrence Creatura

Mill City Press
Minneapolis, MN

Mill City Press, Inc.
322 First Avenue N, 5th floor
Minneapolis, MN 55401
612.455.2293
www.millcitypublishing.com

ISBN-13: 978-1-63413-485-9
LCCN: 2015906535

Cover Design by Jeff Weeks
Typeset by Sophie Chi
Illustrations by John Guzman
Edited by Mark Liu

Printed in the United States of America

For my wife and children-

-Thank you for helping me solve the problem.

I looked into Maria Bartiromo's big, gray, wide-set doe eyes... and fell in. I was paralyzed and mute—a problem, since I was live on CNBC from the floor of the New York Stock Exchange, and she had just asked me a question.

What God had put that strong a brain with that quick a tongue into someone that distractingly attractive? And what person had put an IFB in her ear with a radio link to a team of carnivorous producers who probably spent years on the Yale debate team?

Why did they want to talk with me anyway? Five years before, entering business school, I was a frustrated, cloistered engineer who didn't know the difference between a stock and a bond. I had stumbled into a position as an analyst at an obscure asset management firm and proceeded with an arrogance enabled only by grotesque naiveté. Via a "battlefield promotion" I had become a portfolio manager, ignorant that I was completely out of my depth. But short term performance in the fund was good; relative to competitors' products it had become the "hot dot."

And now I was lost, swimming in Maria's eyes.

With a simultaneous flick of both hands, palms up—a gesture that an Italian grandmother might make—she snapped me awake and I found my tongue. I'm sure I offered the same vacuous nothings that most CNBC guests serve up. Lukewarm porridge for financial minds. I stuttered through all the requisite cliches of that era... "the long term", "the new, new thing", and "monetizing eyeballs" (which today sounds like some sort of grotesque organ-harvesting scheme.) I don't really remember. I began talking too quickly, my forehead beading up with sweat as I realized that hundreds of thousands of people were watching this useless spew. By the time I'd finished, I was certain I had destroyed my career.

They invited me back for next week's show.

Yesterday was my 20th anniversary in this business. Ordinarily, 20 years might not be enough to understand the driving forces of an industry, to describe the tides, to respect the circadian rhythms, to recognize the twin impostors of full-page-spread-in-the-glossy-magazine success and run-on-the-portfolio-collapses-assets-by-eighty-percent failure (I've had both). But these weren't normal years. These years fell into the realm of the old Chinese curse: "May you live in interesting times." Well, it's been an interesting 20 years.

How interesting? We've had valuations round-trip from average levels to never before seen altitudes, only to collapse back again. At its dot-com summit, the S&P 500's price-to-earnings ratio peaked at 44. Value seemed to be irrelevant as price-insensitive retail investors pressed into the market, frothing for "new economy" stocks. One of the editorials in the April 6th, 1999 *Wall Street Journal* was titled simply, "The Good Times Will Last." They didn't.

In horror, we have watched helplessly as some of the historical pillars of the financial industry were nebulized, absorbed, or legislatively emasculated, including Bear Stearns (founded 1928), Lehman Brothers (1850), Merrill Lynch (1914), Fannie Mae (1938), Freddie Mac (1970) and Barings Bank (1762.) Each of these events was a stupefying flashbang to the industry. When J.P. Morgan made a mercy-killing, two-dollar-a-share bid for Bear (the stock had traded at $133 less than a year before), all watched in shock. Bear!?!? Two dollars!?!? Concussed (now former) employees shuffled out of 383 Madison, an octagonal temple of capitalism built just six years prior, with cardboard boxes full of their belongings. They smiled: somebody had taped a $2 bill to the door.

We have had to invest significant time deciphering a metastasizing list of too-clever financial phrases, including soft landings, green shoots, fat fingers, fat tails, black swans, perfect storms, paradigm shifts, change agents, going rogue, decoupling, and kicking the can down the road. It's now probably safe to add to this list "taper," which Federal Reserve wordsmiths believe sounds a lot better than "wind-down"; "retreat", or in the language of military defeat or drug rehab, "withdraw." The perfectly serviceable "I was wondering if you could help me convince people to use our product" has become "I want to reach out and catch you offline to architect an actionable viral strategy, because I don't have the bandwidth to tear down the silos and create something impactful."

We have seen a parade of liars, thieves and frauds. Their names read like the roll call of a dirty, untouchable tribe. Dennis Kozlowski, Joe Nacchio, Michael De Guzman, Anthony Mozillo,

Bernie Madoff, Jerome Kerviel, Allen Sanford, Jeffrey Skilling, Nick Leeson, Joseph Jett, Kenneth Lay, Bernie Ebbers, the Rigas', Richard Scrushy, and the London Whale.

We've endured several different genres of "new normal"—none of which were normal or really new at all. Many of the "new normals" have simply been justifications of bubbles driven by speculative excess. An Internet bubble, a housing bubble, and now a bond bubble. They are normal only in the sense that they follow the tragic path of all bubbles: Creation, inflation, celebration, decimation.

Like an ice cream commercial from Hell, we have confronted 31 flavors of destruction, both natural and man-made, imagined but also all too real. We have had a trans-Pacific tsunami, an Icelandic volcano, explosion of the Deepwater Horizon drilling platform, the Kobe earthquake, Fukishima nuclear disaster, hurricanes Katrina and Sandy, anthrax attacks, Y2K, avian flu, swine flu, mad cow, SARS, Ebola and the Hindenberg omen. Of course, the destruction of the twin towers in September of 2001 by fundamentalist whack-jobs tops the list. Like Obi-Wan Kenobi describing a great disturbance in the force, the loss of those poor souls left the financial industry and the city that housed it riven. To this day, we still haven't really recovered.

So like I said, "interesting times," as the curse would have it.

"There are three ways to make a living in this business," says the partially fictional CEO character in the movie *Margin Call:* "Be first, be smarter, or cheat." This is a book about being smarter.

As for myself, I have been a portfolio manager for more than a decade and a half now. I have invested long and short, conducted research in every economic sector, run funds of every stripe, and developed a budding taste for scotch. I've learned a little bit along the way, and this book is an attempt to share some of those expensive lessons.

It is a "Greatest Hits So Far" album in the middle of a career. Like my career, it is not yet complete, certainly not perfect, and filled with uncertain promise. But hopefully it will enable you, dear reader, to skip a few steps on your own journey.

Contents

Contents

Contents

1. Identify Your Comparative Advantage

"If you don't know who you are, the stock market is an expensive place to find out," said "Adam Smith" (a.k.a. George Goodman.) One important thing you need to learn about yourself is why you would ever expect to be successful in this business.

Much of the time, most stocks are correctly priced. How will you find the small subset for which the price doesn't match the asset? What differentiated, insight-generating skill do you have? Why do you have it? Why will it last? What's so special about you?

Consider the competition. This industry attracts the intellectual Olympians of every discipline on the planet. The best programmers. The best mathematicians. The best strategists. It is said that early expeditions to Mount Everest didn't consult meteorologists about ideal times for a summit bid; they called commodity traders in the agricultural pits. Fund managers compete, and place in, the World Series of Poker. In their spare time they read about the market, trade, or learn obscure Excel functions. Many are abnormal — almost caricatures. Four hours of sleep a day. Musical savants. A near-psychopathic insensitivity to social pressure, conflict, or loss. This is the caliber of the people you are up against.

Early in my career I was sitting at a Bloomberg terminal, screen-gazing with an elder analyst at our firm. At the time he was a god — the sharpest mind in the shop, with wild, gray Einstein hair and a Rainman-like ability to list the smallest details of any company at will. It was the value storm of the late '90s, and portfolio performance had been sputtering for a long time. This particular day was particularly dispiriting — the screen was splashed again in red. That immortal analyst turned to me, looked me directly in the eye, and said, "I feel like a one-legged man in an ass-kicking contest."

Prominent fund manager Bill Miller, who as the owner of the record for most consecutive years of outperformance against the S&P 500 is a person who knows something about kicking financial backsides, believes there are three sources of comparative advantage: 1) informational, 2) analytical and 3) emotional.

Informational advantages, or knowing something that the rest of the world doesn't know, are wonderful to have but difficult to get. The first problem is that the ubiquity and velocity of today's news leaves little room for trading. In the 1980s, academics estimated that after fresh news broke, price adjustments took anywhere from five minutes to two days. Today, prices begin to adjust in seconds, perhaps milliseconds. The other problem is that the government has taken a particularly keen interest in the use of material non-public information. Just ask Raj Rajaratnam. Be prepared to discuss how you came by the whispers of the bid for Bymeout Pharma.

Analytical comparative advantage comes from having the same information as everyone else, but using it differently. This is the ability to come to a more correct conclusion, faster. You could have a stronger brain, or a stronger computer, or maybe you can spot the dissimilar jigsaw puzzle pieces that fit together after all, even though they didn't seem to at first.

Emotional comparative advantage is something else altogether. It comes from within, as your intellectual waters remain calm while others make poor decisions based on panic, greed, extrapolation, and faith. This advantage has more to do with how you are wired and is probably something that is very difficult to learn. Again, who are you?

There are other comparative advantages. Perceptual. Cost. Patience. Speed. Network. Experience. It really doesn't matter which is yours, but it is of existential importance that you have one. Otherwise you are entering the battle unarmed.

2. Quit

Seriously. Think about it. This is really hard. It takes vast amounts of time to do it right. Mistakes can be unforgiving and expensive, and like other specialist professions — prima ballerina, cardiothoracic surgeon, professional wrestler — most people simply don't have the right stuff.

If you are a private investor, do you also fix your own plumbing? Rebuild the transmission on your car? Remove your own gall bladder? Consider the range of your competence relative to the tens of thousands of professional practitioners out there. You can easily hire an expert to do this for you and avoid the risk of a retirement-destroying bobble while simultaneously lowering your blood pressure. With all of your spare time, you can take up the philatelic hobby you always dreamed about.

Or, if you are thinking about trying to enter the industry as a professional, why are you doing it? For the money?

Wrong answer.

With that intention, it's likely you won't succeed. Every portfolio manager I know who is any good is in this for love. When they are onto a good idea, they become animated. Their hands move while they talk, and the wrinkles at the corners of their eyes crease as they smile. This completes them.

What fulfills you? This is an important question because in this business, you simply can't fake it. Can you see yourself wanting to get to work so badly that you speed through traffic, cut sleep to catch the early train, and take stairs on the up escalator two at a time? If not, your best career move may be to never start.

3. There Is No Macro...

...at least not for most of us. If you are a central banker, sure, or if you are paid to do the macro chin-wag thing. You might be a market strategist or a pundit, or perhaps you inhabit the upper management level of a large investment firm. If this is you, then there is a thing called macro. If not, recognize that macro is mostly just raw material for people who get paid to talk.

Interestingly, macroeconomics is a fairly young concept. The aggregation and analysis of economic data was pioneered in the early 20th century by Lord Alfred Keynes, the economist behind the large deficit spending of the Great Depression. Prior to that, the term "macroeconomics" didn't even exist. Now it is taught in every university in the United States as if an economic Wizard of Oz can just pull a macro lever anytime anything economically unpalatable occurs. It is a science that behaves with the certainty of physics but has the track record of alchemy.

Consider the real-world results of some profound top-down lever-pullers: Mao's Great Leap Forward effort toward agricultural collectivization and rapid industrialization (conservative estimate: 18 million dead from starvation); the Nixon administration's temporary wage and price controls (held down prices in the short term only to see inflation explode); the Smoot-Hawley Tariff act of 1930, which raised tariffs across a range of U.S. exports (spawned a global trade war, prolonged and deepened the Great Depression and led to international bank failures including the Vienna-based Creditanstalt, which in turn delivered a timely propaganda victory to a young Austrian politician who took to blaming Jews for all the economic and social troubles of a restless Germany).

With investing, macroeconomics has a similar track record. Capturing economic reward by forecasting macro variables is a strategy available to only a select few individuals, and you and I are not among them. The acquisition of material, non-public geopolitical information is a prerequisite — think of Rothschild's capitalizing on early knowledge of the outcome of the Battle of Waterloo thanks to his carrier pigeons, or George Soros's massive and successful short of the British Pound on England's "Black Wednesday." Or the brokerage accounts of many U.S. senators.

For the rest of us, macro doesn't really exist. If you find yourself in a macroeconomic debate as an investor, stop. You may as well be arguing about religion or politics. Linking your macroeconomic divinations back to an actionable, reliably profitable idea is a low-probability outcome.

But it's even worse than all that. It's not just that your odds of successful macro-forecasting are low. The impact of being wrong is huge. Unlike incorrect microeconomic decisions whose impact is usually limited to an individual company or industry, the blast radius of an incorrect macro decision is vast. It can cut across the whole portfolio. Get this wrong and, like the Titanic, all of your separate compartments will be breached. Nearer My God to Thee, indeed.

Besides, if you are that good at macroeconomic analysis — if you really can correctly forecast interest rates, commodity prices, or the directional changes of the S&P 500 — you don't need this book.

4. A Recommendation: Microeconomics

Macroeconomics is a derivative — a rolling up together of many unique economic decisions. However, such aggregation sacrifices the granularity of information about individual market participants — people, companies, sometimes even entire industries. It is all blurred away. Yet it is within this very information that you are most likely to detect a mismatch between reality and price.

This opposite pole of macroeconomics is microeconomics — or by another name, business. You see, economies don't make decisions. People make decisions. If you can put yourself in their shoes and walk around for a little while, you can anticipate what's next. The stock market, the ultimate anticipation machine, is of course already doing this, but for many companies it does only a cursory job. You can do better.

Walk in people's shoes. Become a company's management for a moment. Does it make sense to increase output? Cut price? Expand internationally? Diversify into a new business? Outsource production? Make an acquisition?

Look at the industry. Is it growing or shrinking? What is the industry structure? Is it consolidated, or are there many participants?

Will the players choose to add capacity? Buy market share with aggressive pricing? Roll up the industry? Sacrifice profit margin to discourage substitutes?

Immerse yourself in the world that management lives in as deeply as possible...deeply enough that you begin to think their thoughts. Then answer these questions.

The power of microeconomics in driving investment returns is well understood on Wall Street. Look at all of the sell-side entities who now deliver channel checks, teen surveys, Chief Information Officer panels, and purchasing manager intentions data; these are just a sliver of the opportunities to gather meaningful intelligence. The full research landscape is unbounded and limited only by your creativity. The sell-side cannot blanket even a fraction of it. Consider it your investing playground.

5. The Financial Press Is Filled With...Journalists

Not CFAs or MBAs or even an online minor in Economics. They are very smart, can write to a deadline, and love a good metaphor if you can spare one. But they don't do the math or even care about the math. They want the narrative, the plot, the story. They live in a verbal world where the numerical realities of a business event are secondary.

Every once in a while there is a dramatic example of this. On August 30, 2010, there was an article on the front page of the bible of capitalism, *The Wall Street Journal*, saying that P/E ratios were losing their relevance in valuing stocks. "As investors focus on the global forces whipsawing the markets, one fundamental measure of stock-market value, the price/earnings ratio, is shrinking in size and importance. And the diminution might not stop for a while." Hmmm. If price and earnings no longer matter, what does? Zip code?

When talking with the wire services, newspaper or online media, I can always tell when they get the pithy supporting quote that they need. They stop asking questions, confirm your title and the spelling of your name and rapidly move to end the conversation. While you are trying to more fully describe the risks and opportunities of a situation, they are pushing the ejector-seat button.

Television is equally bad. Shortly after 9/11 I was in the "green room" of a major network's studio with another portfolio manager, waiting to do an interview about value stocks. It was a nervous time in history; there were still a lot of New Yorkers shuffling saucer-eyed through a fractured, riskier world. Fifteen minutes before our hit time, news flashed across the TV: a white powder, suspected to be anthrax, had been mailed to a television studio.

Well, we were in a television studio. Within seconds, the show's producer walked through the door and simply announced, "I have a wife and kids." And he left. Just left.

In an apparent battlefield promotion, a perspiring Asian girl who looked like a sophomore-year intern sprinted into the room. She was our new producer.

It was clear that five minutes ago, her biggest responsibility was remembering that it was two creams and one sugar. "What do you know about antibiotics?" she panted. The other show guest and I looked at each other and simultaneously confessed that we knew nothing. She pointed to a computer in the corner of the room. "Your hit is in seven minutes — we are going to be talking about antibiotics. There is a computer."

So after seven minutes and the benefit of an Intel Inside x386, 56k dial-up modem, and the Yahoo search engine, yours truly was recommending to the investors of America how to invest in anticipation of waves of citizens moving to protect themselves from an anthrax attack.

Shame on me. But that is the caliber of the great majority of what is on financial TV.

Follow the media's incentives. They are maximizing ratings, not returns. Their value-add is the rapid transmission of raw information. This is entertainment, not analysis. Ingredients, not the meal. Don't use *any* media outlet's conclusions, advice, or insights.

6. What To Study

There are certain educational prerequisites to this profession. Fifth-grade-level math. Twelfth-grade reading comprehension. Fluency in the only true international language (it isn't love): accounting.

After these, things open up when it comes to education.

It's true that many very successful money managers began with a traditional economics/finance course of study. A concentration of others came to the profession via the hard sciences like physics, computer science, mathematics or one of the many flavors of engineering. However, many of the most prominent money managers of recent generations entered the profession through the side door, educationally speaking.

Peter Lynch's most important course of study seemed to be golf — he was a caddy for the president of Fidelity. Bill Gross was a psychology major. David Einhorn has a B.A. in government. Benjamin Graham, George Soros, Bill Miller and Carl Icahn all studied philosophy. Jeffrey Vinik majored in civil engineering. David Abrams, history. Michael Steinhardt, sociology. These curriculum-spanning beginnings suggest that there really isn't an obligatory educational track.

What should you study? After you have mastered the three R's and gotten some letters behind your name, it's pretty open. The easy answer is "everything." Some of your better ideas will come from connecting snippets of disparate evidence from unconnected sources.

Beyond that, learn people. We are all such similar beings, really. There is more difference between a Labrador and a golden retriever than an Australian aborigine and a New York socialite. Learn how to detect ascendancy, deterioration and deceit. Study preferences and influence. Major in mankind.

7. Is Time On Your Side?

As you try to divine the future, recognize that different windows of time offer different opportunities. For example, the phrase "the long term" has different meanings depending on who utters it. To a venture capitalist, it could mean seven years. For a high frequency trader it might mean 300 milliseconds.

Looking across time, some believe that the market has pockets of inconsistency that you can capitalize on. They think that, as different groups of investors discount a company's future cash flows, not all time horizons get the same amount of attention. For this reason the accuracy of pricing is inconsistent and lumpy, depending on the time horizon of these different investor groups.

To oversimplify, let's assume there are only two types of investors: the Yogis, who focus on a five-year horizon, and the Kids, who focus on a five-day horizon and spend the first four days screaming, "Are we there yet?" Imagine these two groups are participating in a market for a company's stock. Because large groups of investors are focused on exactly these two specific time periods, in this scenario it is less likely that the five-day and five-year forecasts for the company are wrong. However, if you were a third type of investor who had the unique ability to invest for six years, perhaps you could spot a ripple in efficient pricing. You are now the only investor even bothering to look beyond year five. The Yogis and the Kids don't care if there is a big contract in year six; it is beyond their horizon and they perceive no benefit from it. But you, with your different horizon, could be discovering a wonderful bargain.

This seems like an oversimplification, but it mirrors the way the industry works. Hedge funds operate on a monthly cycle and are notoriously short-term in perspective. Mutual funds report results quarterly. Because of this, they don't mind if a stock has a bad month but will avoid the exact same stock if the catalyst is more than three months out. Oftentimes longer perspectives aren't priced correctly because they aren't of immediate use to either of these investor groups. Additionally, there may be pockets of mispricing between the patience boundaries of different clumps of investors.

Said another way, different investors assign different durations to the concept of "dead money", that period of wasted time spent waiting for a position to begin working. Look carefully at the spots between and beyond these investor groups' horizons. As a very smart portfolio manager friend of mine likes to say: "All of my stocks have a price/earnings ratio below 10 times — you just have to look at the right year!"

8. Buy The Balance Sheet, Sell The Income Statement

Sometimes my trader makes cat noises. When looking at the price action of a troubled stock which has rebounded, he will often trill "Meow!" implying that the rise we are seeing is, in trader parlance, a "dead cat bounce." This refers to the old trader's theory that, if you drop it from high enough, even a dead cat will bounce.

Translated from cat language, my trader is saying that the rebound is only temporary, and that the stock is likely to resume its descent. This is a risky decision point. How can you increase your safety when considering a declining stock?

When participating in risky activities such as walking a tightrope, swinging on the trapeze, or buying stocks, it is important to have a safety net. With stocks, the safety net begins with a company's balance sheet, and your research should start here.

Look carefully at that plunging stock. Yes, you don't want to catch a falling knife, but recognize that it is safe to pick one up off the ground. The balance sheet is bedrock. It describes what a company is made of. When you're purchasing a stock, this is what you're buying...what you will own. It is your backstop during times of trouble and your raw material for future success. Buy this at a fair price and you are off to a good start.

So now fast-forward. Some time has passed since your purchase of the stock. If you're fortunate enough to be successful with your investment, the balance sheet will fade in importance. Now you will have enjoyed the double-barrel blessings of both earnings and multiple expansion. Nobody cares anymore about the market value of that empty lot in Menlo Park. No, now it's all about the income statement, and at this stage you will need to locate the next purchasers of the stock. You'll recognize them: they will be frothy and looking for future growth. Sell them your income statement.

9. Never Do Business With Anyone Who Calls You "Dude"

Just don't.

10. Avoid Round Numbers

On average, others won't. Don't set a limit of $20 when $19.96 will work. It's not that you will have the precision to pinpoint value with this degree of accuracy, but something else entirely. Using this tip will help you avoid the gaggle of investors who are sucked in by the gravitational pull of a round number.

Someone once asked NHL god Wayne "The Great" Gretzky what made him so great. His reply: "I always skated to where the puck was going to be." You can mimic this strategy by taking advantage of the pockets of liquidity that lurk just outside the comfort and certainty of a nice, neat integer.

Our brains take many shortcuts so we can process faster and come to conclusions more quickly. "Behavioral Economics" is an entirely separate field of study which describes some of these shortcuts and evolutionary leftovers. Perhaps this is one of them, or perhaps it's just plain laziness, but people tend to round to the nearest whole number. You shouldn't.

11. The Two Ingredients For Investment Success

1) Be Different
2) Be Correct

The challenge of ingredient 1 is to figure out if what you believe is materially different from what the consensus really is. You may have acquired better information before the competition, but if it isn't significantly different from what others already think, you don't have anything.

You can't know different until you've determined same. Like navigating with a map, if you don't know where you are, you will have a tough time determining where you are going. Where is the consensus anchored — mathematically but also perceptually? Current expectations aren't always expressed through earnings or revenue forecasts alone. Timing of new product introductions, use of cash flow, dividend rates, management transitions, and divestitures are all expectations, too.

British economic deity John Maynard Keynes once likened consensus-hunting to a fictional newspaper contest in which photos of six young women were published in the paper, and readers would pick the prettiest face among them. (It was the 1930s, OK? And maybe we haven't come that far anyway when you consider Mark Zuckerberg's precursor to Facebook was "Facemash", a virally popular hot-or-not website that ranked female students based on attractiveness.) The winner of Keynes's hypothetical competition would not be the woman herself but the *reader* who picked the woman who ultimately received the most votes.

Keynes realized that this wasn't a competition to pick the face that he thought prettiest, but rather to pick the face who *most others* thought was the one. While a naive competitor might select the woman he believed was most attractive, more astute readers would chose the woman who had the most conventional beauty. Even more sophisticated voters might adjust for both groups and come up with a third-order estimation. So the question changes from "what do you think?" to "what do you think others will think?", and even to "what do you think others will think about what others think?" And so on.

Participants would see that the game is not really about the women at all. Instead, it is about forecasting readers' preferences and perceptions. The stock market is similar, and if you have a sense for which beauty is likely to be picked, you are now ready to be different.

Different comes from within. It takes curiosity, reason, intellect, hustle, creativity, confidence, suspicion, the strength to be non-accepting, and a willingness to stand alone. Not a common combination of attributes.

Also, being different is not enough. The second and final ingredient for investment success is to be correct. Being different and incorrect can be spectacularly disastrous: *Oh, the humanity!* This book will help you become correct more often.

And how will you know if you're correct? *That's* the easy part. The market will let you know.

12. If You Sit Too Long, You Will Forget How To Dance

There is an unwritten rule in engineering which says that 18 months after you depart your profession, your knowledge becomes outdated, and your ability to perform in your field of study fades. So it is with investing — our skills are perishable. Like an athlete or a musician, the daily routine of training, evolving long-term patterns of muscle memory, and getting your brain ahead (but not too far ahead) of what your body is doing is a continuous process that doesn't benefit from spending a year in Tahiti finding yourself.

It isn't just that your knowledge fades (it does). It's also that you lose the ability to counterbalance management's hopeful vision of the future against the stark, heartless criticism required to properly vet an idea. It is at the intersection of these two perspectives where prices are set. If you're rusty, you are going to fall off the balance beam.

More than once I've seen the veteran, back from sabbatical, try to re-enter the fray too soon. They always seem a little too sunny. The scars left by their investment mistakes have healed too thoroughly and they tend to make errors driven by overconfidence and optimism. Distance yourself from them until they find the ground again.

13. Know The Short Side

First of all, before this chapter really gets underway, a quick alert: This is probably the most important tip in this book. Administer it liberally, as if you were employing the antidote to a poison!

Owning a stock is like a relationship. The commitment that comes from a deep love is what great fortunes and great marriages are made from. Unfortunately, the longer your relationship lasts, the more likely you are to lose objectivity. There is nothing wrong with having passion for an idea, but recognize that the things that you do when you like a stock — repeat the hypothesis to others, gather confirming observations, commit capital to it — leave you imbalanced. When you are in love, if things begin to go wrong, at first you will not see it. A prominent short seller once stated his value-add thusly: "The reason I am successful is that people consistently underestimate how bad things can get."

The way to inoculate yourself from this risk is to become knowledgeable in the other side of the trade — the "short story." Make it your goal to become fully fluent in the short side and to simultaneously repeat the short arguments every time you impart the long pitch.

Researchers say that we remember 10 percent of what we hear, 20 percent of what we read and 80 percent of what we say and do. Learn the short hypothesis. Write it. Speak it. Teach it. When you can look at your audience and see them just as taken by your reasons why a stock will go up as why it will decline, you know you are at a point of intellectual stasis. You are now ready to make the next decision correctly.

Heed the observation from John Stuart Mill's *On Liberty:* "He who knows only his own side of the case, knows little of that."

14. The Scoreboard Doesn't Lie

One of the blessings of this profession is that it is easy to measure performance. This isn't the case in most enterprises, where evaluating a person's output involves incomplete, flawed and amorphous metrics only partially linked to organizational success. Customer satisfaction, increased sales, and making more huffofenators per hour are all honorable goals, but each can be delivered with tactics that damage the organism as a whole.

In the early '90s, management of a large U.S. automaker decided to emulate its Japanese competitor's just-in-time production systems. They wanted leaner work-in-process inventories, so they measured employees based on their ability to keep inventory counts low at the end of each month. Result? On the day before every month-end, employees loaded excess inventory onto trucks and dumped it into the Detroit River. One employee said you could walk to Windsor, Canada, on the partially submerged parts.

In recent years, in an effort to improve the measurement of employee performance, all sorts of alternative, floofy, new-age metrics have been dreamt up. DISC analysis (Drive, Influence, Steadiness, Compliance), MBO (Management by Objective...

inventory reduction, anyone?) and the Orwellian 360 degree review are examples. The existence of these performance measurement contortions is proof of how hard this is to do.

Our profession is different. None of these problems exist in the sphere of investment management. You get a number at the end of every day. Performance calculations are easy, and you learned all the math required to make them before the end of fifth grade.

When using a concrete accounting system to measure performance, you create raw material that can reveal your weaknesses, confirm the sanity of uncomfortable but successful strategies, and serve as a gauge and proof statement of your competence.

The scoreboard is your teacher, referee, disciplinarian and critic. Be honest about what it is telling you.

15. Fish From A Stocked Pond

Whether you are choosing an invasion strategy, which bar to go to on Friday night, or what group of stocks to look at, it is important to have a target-rich environment.

The stock market is a losers' game. A commonly used metaphor is that it is a casino, and you are the gambler — the odds are structurally stacked against you. This is why, over time, a majority of active managers underperform their benchmarks. You don't have to be one of them. The first step is to shift the probabilities in your favor before you even begin.

Your goal should be to alter the ecology of the stock market. Reduce the number of stocks you consider while increasing the quality of the ideas you look at. Put yourself in a situation where you are more likely to catch a fish! Some examples on the long side: small stocks, value stocks and momentum stocks are all supported by bodies of academic evidence that suggest they produce better than average returns over time.

Choosing what not to look at is just as important. Some entire asset classes are poisonous. Small-cap growth comes to mind.

Look at the long-term data: the headwinds here are strong. With this group of stocks, the good times are very good — but so much capital is vaporized during the bad times that you will have trouble keeping up.

Certain industries can also be difficult. Early stage biotech? These cash-flow-negative lottery tickets are dubious, and unless you are a geneticist or have an uncle in a clinical trial who went from terminal to dancing the funky chicken, it probably makes sense to cast your line in ponds where there are more fish.

16. Don't Get Framed

Researchers David Kahneman and Amos Tversky once presented a group of subjects with the following personality profile and question:

Linda is 31 years old, single, outspoken, and very bright. She majored in philosophy. As a student, she was deeply concerned with issues of discrimination and social justice and also participated in anti-nuclear demonstrations.

Subjects were then asked which of the following two statements is more probable.

Statement A: Linda is a bank teller.
Statement B: Linda is a bank teller who is active in the feminist movement.

Which of these do you think is more likely?

86% of those asked chose "B", which is the wrong answer. This is because as you stack conditions one upon another, each filters out more and more people. The group "bank tellers" is always

39

larger than "bank tellers who are feminists", which is larger than "bank tellers who are feminists who have blue eyes." So why did almost nine out of ten people get this wrong?

It is the framing to the question that throws everyone. The prelude describing Linda triggers our brain's pre-loaded constructs, and from that moment our perceptions warp and misperceive reality. We no longer see things as they are, but rather as we *think* they are.

Framing is often used by salespeople. Did you ever have a realtor lead you to a few imperfect properties before showing you the one that you eventually purchased? Have you been framed at a car dealership? During your last visit to an electronics retailer? In any situation where there is a consultative sale with a sales agent, framing is a tool that the merchant can choose to use.

Of course a lot of consultative selling occurs in the world of investing. Do you find any of your investment ideas by word of mouth? Prepare to be framed, and keep your anti-framing defenses handy.

Make it a habit to separate the question being asked (Is Linda a bank teller and a feminist?, Is this stock inexpensive?) from the surrounding information which is offered (anti-nuclear demonstrator, the shares have declined.) Look at the question alone: how would you go about answering it?

Perhaps most important, give yourself time. The reason framing works is that in a rush to reach a conclusion, we offhandedly accept reasoning from others, even those who have different and sometimes opposing financial incentives than our own. Be conscious of your information sources and give yourself some moments to think independently of them.

17. See The Company Within The Company

Stagnant, troubled or moribund companies oftentimes reinvent themselves and unexpectedly rise from the dead. (Examples from recent history: IBM, Apple, Netflix, General Electric.) This is simply a consequence of human nature. Management teams are adaptive problem solvers, and most spend a lot of their downtime using deep industry-specific knowledge to dream up ways to prevent their own extinction.

As they scramble for relevance, a new company can be born within the original. It will have a different character than the old company. It will produce something in high demand by customers. It will likely have higher margins. It will grow rapidly.

Because of relative growth rates alone, it will evolve to become a significant if not dominant portion of the business. However, in the beginning at least, it will also go largely unnoticed by investors.

There are two reasons why investors often miss the change. The first is a form of voluntary blindness. If in high school you played soccer, basketball, lacrosse, or any other team sport as badly as I did, then you know all about this. You were the person your teammate would look at, see wide open and unguarded, and then turn away from to look for someone else to pass to. We used to call this being "looked off."

Professionally, we look off companies all the time. There are literally thousands of candidates for investment, time is scarce, and it is simply much easier to just go with our preconceptions. Why kiss the frog when you can choose anyone else in the kingdom? If you take one thing from this chapter, take this: It is not in spite of but *because* of these broadly shared preconceptions that an investment opportunity exists.

The second problem is that even if we did grudgingly decide to look at this boring, old, declining, afterthought of a company, we don't notice or price the change going on within. We don't value the new business, investigate its growth trajectory, perform SWOT and Porter analysis. We just see a dying company with a cute anecdote attached. What we should spot instead is a company evolving toward a crossroad where the smaller, more exciting, rapidly growing business will in time come to define the firm. This occurs at an ever-increasing rate as the growing new unit becomes a larger slice of the pie.

IBM sold meat slicers, scales and coffee grinders. Samsung was a grocer and noodle manufacturer. Lamborghini made tractors. Wipro's name used to be Western India Vegetable Products Ltd. Nintendo made playing cards. Nokia had three product lines: rubber, cable and paper. Shell Oil was a retailer and importer of collectible seashells.

Things change.

See the company within the company. Value it. Add it to your value for the old company. Compare the sum to today's share price. Voila! You may have just found a mispricing.

18. Always Look Around The Corner

Company management teams know the question you are about to ask. In fact, they have already answered it hundreds of times for new and potential investors — so much so that they barely perceive you as an individual person but rather as a member of a predictable species: Analyst.

Think this isn't true? Watch their body English as you ask. They have stopped listening to you as soon as they match your inquiry with one of their practiced responses. They have shifted from listening to talking posture (straighter back, eyes wider, hands moving) and probably have begun speaking before you have even finished your question.

But it's even worse than all that. Companies are increasingly controlling and binding their communications until all spontaneity, granularity, and incremental information is bled from the conversation. During today's company conference calls, most management teams have scripted answers to anticipated questions before the call even begins. A growing number of companies are even pre-recording their call's opening commentary. Even though it's a "live" call, that is a tape of the CEO's voice you are hearing. And while you're listening, she's deciding which call participants will be allowed to ask questions. (Hint: Sell-side firms with "buy" ratings and branded long-only shops who are existing holders need only apply; otherwise, don't bother pressing "3" to ask a question.)

In this world where differentiated information is getting ever more scarce, the structure of your questions can make all the difference. If you have a face-to-face meeting with management, don't waste it. After they give you their off-the-shelf answer to question A subsection b, ask your next question on the same subject. Then hit the same spot again. During one extended back-and-forth exchange, an unusually compassionate CEO once instructed one of my co-workers: "If you ask the right question, I can give you the answer you are looking for." Drill deep and you might learn something that others don't know.

For example, consider this somewhat hypothetical conversation about a commonly discussed subject, share repurchase:

Q: I noticed your recent share repurchase authorization. Could you talk —

A: (interrupting) "The $125 million reaffirms our commitment to creating shareholder value. We remain confident in the fundamental strength of our business, including our ability to generate cash flow to support continued growth and to create value for shareholders through the combination of dividends and opportunistic share repurchases. We are authorized to repurchase shares from time to time in the open market or in privately negotiated transactions. The timing and amount of stock repurchases will depend on a variety of factors, including market conditions as well as corporate and regulatory considerations..." Blah blah, blah blather, blah boilerplate... "This combined with the remainder of our previous authorization totals over $125 million."

Q: Could you talk about how you plan to implement the program?

A: "The timing and amount of repurchase will vary based on a variety of factors. We are committed to increasing shareholder value."

Q: Yes but can you talk about how you plan to mechanically execute the program? Are you price sensitive? Will you target a certain number of shares or dollar amount per day? Many companies first do a large percentage of their authorization quickly, then decelerate. Others authorize but never purchase a share. What will you do?

A: "I think you will see us more active at certain price levels."

Q: How do you choose these levels?

A: "Management and the board identify levels of significance."

Q: How does that conversation go? Does it begin at the board level or is management making the call? Who initiates the discussion?

A: "It typically begins with management although we have a strong board and we make sure that we have venues where all voices are expressed."

And so on...

In this example, rather than just hearing about the company's delightful new share repurchase program (the outline of which was already described in the press release that you read prior to the meeting), you now have some other valuable information. You now know that balance sheet willing, $125 million of capital will be used to defend the stock at lower price points, increasing your margin of safety as an investor. You also know that management is calling the shots, and that the board, while consulted, is not driving. This revelation has many implications beyond just share repurchase.

When going on any exploration, be it a physical journey or a research meeting, you won't discover anything worthwhile if you don't go far enough. Go beyond the trail others have worn. Ask the next question. Look around the corner.

19. Hitch A Ride

There are many changes occurring in the world at any moment, and many companies are taking bleeding-edge risks to drive those changes forward. However, there is also a second class of companies hitching a ride on the coattails of the same change, but with a lower exposure to risk. Like a remora suckerfish latched onto a shark, they are attached to bigger, fast-moving and powerful trends, but they aren't the trend itself. These firms are along for the ride.

Every era has trends worth latching onto. In 1848, shiny metal flakes were found in the tailrace of John Sutter's lumber mill and a gold rush was born. The big trend was gold fever, and we all know the rest of the story, but notice that today you would have trouble naming a single gold miner who benefitted from the high-risk gold mining trend.

The hitchhikers — those who sold supplies and services to the miners — are a different story. Before setting off, prospectors bought their wheelbarrows from "Wheelbarrow Johnny" — John Studebaker. The German who sold them canvas for tents was Levi Strauss. Their outpost banker, Wells Fargo. The Italian immigrant who sold sweets from his tent you know today as Ghirardelli. These are the survivors of the huge gold exploration mega-trend. It is the hitchhikers we still know today, while the miners' names and fortunes have faded into the dust of history.

Today's '49ers are blessed with a world awash in exciting and rapidly growing mega-trends. Examples: Increasing bandwidth consumption, aging baby boomers, a shifting preference for private-label goods, structurally lower natural gas costs in North America, increased protein consumption in emerging markets, alternative channels for distribution of entertainment content, increasing frequency of food consumption away from home, designer pharmaceuticals customized to an individual's genetic makeup, and the commercialization of nanotechnology, to name just a few.

Competition at the tip of the spear in these industries is fierce, risky and unforgiving. The front end will see a lot of casualties. (Another late 19th century bit of wisdom: "You can always recognize the pioneers. They are the ones with an arrow sticking out of their chests!") However, anywhere you see a sustainable trend, you can ride it with lower risk. Pick up a hitchhiker.

20. Find Evergreens

On January 29th, 2000, the fruits of a four-year criminal antitrust investigation into the art market were revealed on the front page of the *Financial Times*. The headline blared: CHRISTIE'S ADMITS FIXING COMMISSIONS: AUCTION HOUSE TELLS THE U.S. JUSTICE DEPARTMENT THAT IT MADE A DEAL WITH SOTHEBY'S.

Shares of Sotheby's, a public company, immediately began plummeting. The following month, chairman A. Alfred Taubman and CEO Diana "DeDe" Brooks resigned, and on April 13, 2001, a judge accepted a $512 million joint agreement between the two auction houses to end a class-action lawsuit on behalf of 130,000 buyers and sellers. Taubman offered to pay $156 million of the Sotheby's portion of the settlement out of his own pocket.

Just over a year later, Taubman was sentenced to a one-year jail term and an additional $7.5 million fine. By then, the stock had lost almost half its value, but the story wasn't over. The stain on the business remained and this — combined with a weakening art market — drove further declines. Investors watched in horror as the shares force-marched to just over $7. From the first appearance of the *Financial Times* article, Sotheby's stock had collapsed 74%.

By all appearances, this stock — and company — seemed doomed. But even a simple analysis suggested otherwise.

Some companies enjoy a sustainable competitive advantage that allows them to harvest high returns in a low-risk fashion for extended periods of time. The nature of the advantage can vary — it can be a patent, a customer base with high exit costs, a secret recipe, control of a unique geological asset, or some other lasting, special and valuable attribute.

It is important to recognize that these firms are not like other companies. Think of them as being in a separate evergreen category, although most other investors won't.

Most of the time this higher-caste status will not be important. However, during the rare moments when the evergreen stock has a hiccup, it will mean everything. During these times, many investors will overweight temporary bad news and momentarily overlook the power and durability of the evergreen's unique advantage. At this point, you will be hearing the cacophony of a short-term informational free-for-all. Ignore it. Zoom out and see what the company really *is*.

During the Sotheby's scandal, here's what people priced: DOJ investigation. A large and certain penalty. Controlling shareholder in jail. Uncertain and volatile short-term earnings.

Here's what the company was: an evergreen. In existence since

1744. A brand trusted by the affluent classes to handle some of their largest and most sensitive assets. A firm whose services are often contracted repeatedly over decades by multiple generations of the same family. A relationship-based business whose employees are confidantes of the customer. A firm which is a member of a duopoly controlling 90% of the world's major art sales with natural (and most of the time legal) pricing power. A business whose customers are less affected by economically difficult times. An industry with incredibly high barriers to entry.

Eventually investors re-discovered Sotheby's evergreen nature. Five years after the depths of the price-fixing investigation, it had risen over 700%. Yes, the share price had waffled, but the essence of the company had never changed.

21. Watch *The Karate Kid* Again

Within this coming-of-age tale about a whiny boy who looks like a stick insect is a hidden message; you may have missed it, but this is actually a movie about investing. Some of the more relevant quotes:

"Wax on wax off"
One day in 1970, Secretary of State Henry Kissinger burst into Chief of Staff H.R. Haldeman's office with aerial reconnaissance photos of construction at a Cuban seaport. He animatedly pointed to one of the photos showing that soccer fields were being installed. Haldeman was mystified. "Soccer fields, so what?" Haldeman said. Kissinger exclaimed, "Cubans play baseball. *Russians* play soccer! Those soccer fields could mean war — I need to see the president *now!*"

The Russians were in Cuba. Most everyone would only have seen playing fields, but Kissinger saw early symptoms of a coming confrontation between superpowers.

The point is, seemingly aimless and unrelated things can strengthen you in unexpected ways. A breadth of skills, knowledge and experience can help you link disparate elements and reach a higher level of perception more quickly than others.

The power of linking apparently purposeless actions is also revealed in the commencement speech which Steve Jobs gave to the graduating class of Stanford in 2005. He described the unfulfilling beginnings of his own brief college experience. Unsure off his career path and feeling guilty about wasting his family's money, he dropped out. But the act of dropping out gave him the freedom to sneak into classes he was interested in, rather than attending ones previously mandated. It was here that he wandered into a calligraphy class, which he took for no other reason than that it intrigued him. This pointless choice, 10 years later, became the foundation for the multiple typefaces and proportionally spaced fonts which helped differentiate the first Macintosh.

Jobs observed that it was this, along with many other unscripted events in his life (getting fired from Apple, being diagnosed with terminal pancreatic cancer) that made all the difference. These led — in an aimless, unplanned and circuitous route — to the success which characterized his career.

So spread yourself out. Investigate seemingly irrelevant passions. Learn from your cab driver, people from the opposite political pole, artists, scientists, poets, janitors. This differentiating body of knowledge will be a source of higher understanding.

"Lesson on balance not only for Karate. For whole life."
If you push too hard in this profession, you can get lost. Don't get too far over your skis. I've known people who slept on cots

in their offices in order to get more work done. However, I have noticed no correlation between office sleeping and investment performance.

For most of us mortals, hard work is a toll we pay in exchange for success in the industry. But there are limits, and the returns to being correct are greater than the returns to working hard. Don't risk the former by overdoing the latter.

Hard work is just one example. Psychological distortions can occur from too much of anything. A monoculture of thought carries large and even inevitable risks. Look closely at the industry. It is not owned by the smartest, or the hardest working, or the most politically savvy. These are partial prerequisites, but the masters are those who wield a quiver of complimentary assets. There is a long list of means that might be at your disposal: Intuition. Self-confidence. Patience. Thrift. Insight.

There are many more... Use a combination of the weapons that you possess, and stay balanced.

"Man who catch fly with chopstick achieve anything."
"Ever catch one?"
"Not yet."
Take a moment to imagine success. What are your personal and professional goals? Not your small aspirations, but rather what does the lottery win look like? Visualize this for a moment.

The truth, of course, is that you may not make it to this personal nirvana. But for the moment, so what? The path ahead is still very clear: Keep trying. The investment equivalent of "The journey is the destination" philosophy is an accumulation of industry wisdom that will make you a more accurate decision maker, and it is likely that this pattern of single-minded effort will get you to higher professional altitudes.

"What kind of belt do you have?"
"Canvas. JC Penny. $3.98. You like?"
In the pure search for investment returns, academic degrees mean little. Yes, classroom training can give you some tools, but it is how you wield them that matters. There are certainly many examples where the exoskeleton of academic pedigree offered no protection from financial carnage. Roger Lowenstein's book *When Genius Failed* is a modern tragedy describing how an academic A-Team with degrees from Harvard, MIT, Stanford and University of Chicago, whose members including a Vice Chairman of the Federal Reserve, several professors, and two Nobel Prize laureates, (spoiler alert here)...failed. When you look at their portfolio just before its collapse, "genius" isn't the first word that comes to mind: 25:1 leverage on just under $5 billion in equity, with $1.2 trillion (yes, trillion with a "t") in notional derivative value off balance sheet. At the time, the firm's implosion destabilized the entire global financial system.

In contrast, look at the anti-heroes of another book, Michael Lewis's *The Big Short,* which describes an unrelated gaggle of investors who successfully navigated the housing bubble. They included a one-eyed heavy-metal fan with Asperger's syndrome. Two guys who set up a hedge fund in their garage. An abrasive lawyer-turned-analyst-turned-manager. True, all of them had some level of academic training, but that wasn't their currency. These were the outsiders, the investment industry's equivalent of the *Star Wars* bar scene. They were the handful, among the hundreds of thousands of professional investors, who spotted and executed the biggest trade of a generation.

Beware taking shortcuts with social signals such as college degree, employment history, awards received, or fame in general. Also bury all of your preconceptions. You won't be served well by believing the stereotype: the paunchy man with the "aw-shucks" southern drawl, the blonde with hair a bit too tall and heels a bit too high, the quiet new employee with pimples. You don't want to be the one to find out, too late, that they are the smartest people in the room.

"No such thing as bad student, only bad teacher. Teacher say, student do."
Choose your teachers, and teaching materials, carefully. What you watch, read, and listen to is the primordial pool from which you will arise. Recognize that a variety of potential educators may have vastly different incentives than your own. Some of their goals include improving viewership, avoiding embarrassment, increasing trading volume, getting a promotion, selling books, boosting ratings, or simply retaining their job. If you encounter "teachers" with these goals, understand that — for all of them — your investment success is unimportant.

"Sweep the leg"
Just kidding. Don't sweep the leg.

22. Ignore Tempters

In the play *Murder In the Cathedral,* Thomas Becket waits for his own assassination, which he knows is coming. On his last night, he is visited by four tempters. Each offers a reward — physical safety, fame and riches, political power, the self-serving pride of martyrdom — if Becket diverts from his singular focus on God. All of these rewards are attractive and desirable outcomes, and yet none are Becket's mission. So he refuses the tempters, and although it didn't quite work out for Thomas at the time (he was slain), he is an immortal in history, a saint, all because of his unwavering focus.

Focus is important. But you will find you are not immune to the pathologies that can drag you away from a single-mindedness required for investment success. Some of these tempters are very attractive, and they can cause you to stray.

The analogies to other professions are many and are the stuff of great morality tales: the boxer who wins the big fight only to develop a gambling problem; the unknown singer who gets the big record contract but then discovers drugs; the altruistic politician brought low by a corrosive town.

It's not much different with investing, but the temptations are perhaps more subtle. The lure can be concealed in a false teacher's charisma, a slight shift in how others perceive you, or your own internal whispers of self-protection. Be careful. Don't let false rewards divert your focus.

23. Golden Nugget

Is gold an asset class, money, or a commodity? A store of value, a barbarous relic, a deadweight loss to any portfolio? These are religious questions. I pass on only what an old-timer imparted to me as I was entering the business: *"Put 10% of your assets in gold and pray that it never works."*

24. An Ode To Small Cap Value

In the sport of investing, you can compete anywhere. But there is one corner of the market where the sun shines more often. It is the southwest corner of the style box landscape, where small size and low valuation intersect.

The small cap value asset class has lasting and unappreciated advantages. Foremost are the small cap and value effects, two academically proven phenomena which suggest that over time, inexpensive small stocks outperform. These effects have been shown to occur in different time periods, exchanges, and geographies, and have continued ex-post...that is, they have continued to be effective after having been discovered.

Similar to the way a retriever is different from a pit bull which is still different from a Chihuahua, small value stands out by its very nature. The small-cap effect and value effect are part of what the asset class *is.* Long-term outperformance is part of its character.

Another driver of small value returns is merger and acquisition activity. Most larger companies, in their search for growth, openly discuss their desire to deploy cash flows "strategically." Organic growth rates of most mature businesses simply aren't exciting enough to capture the attention of investors, so M&A becomes the salve. A disproportionate number of acquisition targets inhabit the small-value space because they are both the right size and the right price.

Long-term return data supports small value as a sweet spot of the market. Over time, with compounding, the asset class simply outruns all others. This is why if you look at a multi-decade performance chart of small value compared to other asset classes, you will notice that they use a logarithmic scale on the return axis. Do you remember your logarithms? Why don't they just use a normal linear grid — you know, the type of graph that you learned how to build in the fourth grade? Answer: because the other major asset classes lag so far behind, you wouldn't be able to tell them apart otherwise.

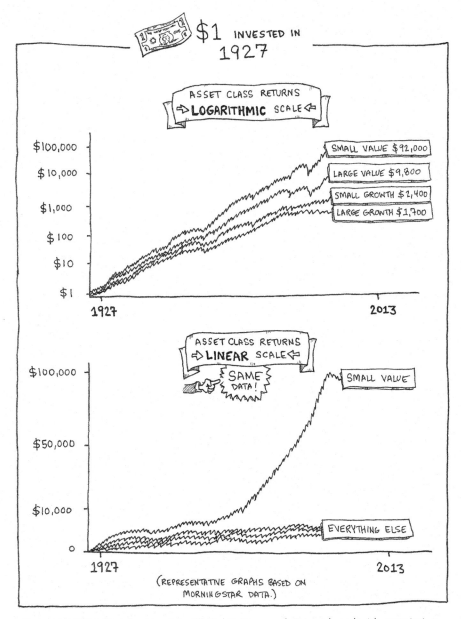

$1 INVESTED IN 1927

ASSET CLASS RETURNS
LOGARITHMIC SCALE

SMALL VALUE $92,000
LARGE VALUE $9,800
SMALL GROWTH $2,400
LARGE GROWTH $1,700

ASSET CLASS RETURNS
LINEAR SCALE

SAME DATA!

SMALL VALUE

EVERYTHING ELSE

(REPRESENTATIVE GRAPHS BASED ON MORNINGSTAR DATA.)

Imagine you're in a baseball game and for each at-bat, the pitcher throws every pitch in the sweet spot of the strike zone. This is the essence of small value. It isn't going to change, and that is why you should expect honorable returns from the asset class to continue over the long term. If you're looking for a place to find stocks that will outperform, consider starting here.

25. Gift Of The Cognoscenti

When, in a moment of benevolence, the investing gods determined to bestow a gift to investors, they created experts. Experts help form mass opinions, and at times they can be deliciously incorrect. This is often where "different" is born. Consider these expert forecasts:

"I think there is a world market for maybe five computers."
- Chairman of IBM, 1943

"Man will not fly for 50 years."
-Wilbur Wright, 1901

"We don't like their sound, and guitar music is on the way out."
- Decca Recording Co., rejecting The Beatles, 1962

"Television won't last because people will soon get tired of staring at a plywood box every night."
Darryl Zanuck, 20th Century Fox, 1946

"There is no reason for any individual to have a personal computer in their home."
Ken Olsen, president, Digital Equipment Corp., 1980

"The [atom] bomb will never go off, and I speak as an expert in explosives."
-Admiral William Leahy to President Truman, 1945

"With over fifteen types of foreign cars already on sale here, the Japanese auto industry isn't likely to carve out a big share of the market for itself."
-*Business Week*, 1968

"*There are ominous signs that the Earth's weather patterns have begun to change dramatically and that these changes may portend a drastic decline in food production — with serious political implications for just about every nation on Earth.*"
- *Newsweek* magazine article on global cooling, "The Cooling World", 1975

"Prices on electric cars will continue to drop until they're within the reach of the average family."
- *The Washington Post*, 1915

"*Dow 40,000: Strategies for Profiting from the Greatest Bull Market in History*"
- title of book by David Elias, published 6 months before the Dow peaks, then plummets.

"By 2005 or so, it will become clear that the Internet's impact on the economy has been no greater than the fax machine's."
-Paul Krugman, *New York Times* economist, 1998

"*Stock prices have reached what looks like a permanently high plateau...I expect to see the stock market a good deal higher*

than it is today within a few months."
- Irving Fischer, the most prominent economist of his day, eight days before the 1929 crash

Regard all expert opinion with equal measures of criticism and suspicion. At the end of the day, an expert is really only someone who is well dressed, more than five miles from home, and paid to talk.

26. Don't Cheat

If you are any good at research, at some point in your career you will have the opportunity to cheat. Don't do it.

Cheating comes in a variety of degrees, from actively malicious to accidentally opportunistic. Regardless of which flavor you choose, the odds of success are increasingly not in your favor.

Quick quiz: What is the difference between true love and email?

Answer: Email lasts forever.

The longevity and mass of electronic data that track your actions are matched only by the seemingly infinite time and expense that today's investigators are willing to invest to catch you. And this is only the least important reason not to cheat.

A more important reason is what it does to you psychologically. You see, cheating has a positive feedback loop. After you make that initial moral slip, six armed federal agents do not break down the door and Mirandize you. No, the problem is, the first thing that happens is good. You make more money, get the promotion, become more famous. Immediately your subconscious learns that cheating = good. So you do it again. And again. Eventually it becomes a habit... and then an infection.

I have an FBI agent friend who spends some time working undercover. He described one sting where the target, a drug dealer, looked across a table with a heaping $120,000 cash on it and saw...cops. The dealer wasn't dumb. He correctly spotted the setup and got out of there, quickly.

As he walked out of the hotel room, he turned to my (still trusted) friend and announced, "Those guys are f***ing cops," then got into his car in the parking garage. He started the car, but instead of driving away he waited. Fifteen minutes later he turned the car off, returned to the room, did the deal, and was promptly arrested. It was all recorded perfectly on camera. Despite the fact that he basically knew he was selling drugs to the police, he still went ahead. His simple reason, stated to an agent after the jig was up: "I had to do it." He did it because cheating is an addiction. At its very heart, it is corrosive.

Morally, cheating is wrong. It is theft. It destroys lives. Just because financial crimes are non-violent and victims are often distant, it doesn't make them any less awful. I met with Enron's pension consultant on the day of the firm's collapse, shortly after he left the building. Many employees, in addition to having their livelihoods derived from the company, also had imprudently oversized portions of their life savings tied up in Enron stock. The consultant looked like the shell-shocked bystander standing next to the crater left by a suicide bomber.

"What's it like over there?" I asked.

His reply: "People are sitting on the floors in the hallways, crying."

You don't want to be a person who does this to others. This is the most important reason not to cheat.

27. Find A Mentor

If you work in an investment firm, identify the best stock-picker in the house and become his or her understudy. Watch them think. Understand how they weight different uncertainties. Learn how they choose the next question to ask. Shadow their intellectual footwork.

You will be trying to poach some accrued wisdom. Now, there isn't a lot of time for charity during working hours, so it won't come free. Luckily, all investment professionals suffer from a common problem, and you can be the solution. Every potential mentor will have the curse of having more ideas than time. In the Internet age, information is now near infinite. Herein lies your opportunity. You can investigate minutiae and lateral themes that your mentor otherwise wouldn't have the time to explore. Do this without being asked.

Not working at an investment firm? Find other ways to access mentors. Who would you like to emulate? Munger, Miller, Klarman, Burry, Vinick, Whitman, Paulson, Lynch, Dalio? Each has a body of work you can study. Pay particular attention to their biases, failures, and periods of underperformance — these are where the wiring that makes them successful is often best revealed. Let this be your graduate school.

28. Good Ideas Are Like Rainbows

They are infrequent: Most of the people I talk to say that if you can find two or three genuinely good ideas a year, you are doing well.

They are temporary: The half-life of a good idea depends on the source of the mispricing, but you won't know its duration in advance. The shot clock is running, but you can't see it. Make haste.

They only occur under certain conditions: Think illiquidity/distress/confusion/misunderstanding/chaos/discomfort.

They can be incomplete: You won't always have all the information you want. Maybe you don't have visibility on the full arc of the idea. That doesn't mean it isn't a good notion.

They are beautiful: Just try to describe your favorite idea without smiling.

At their end lies a pot of gold.

29. Find Colonel Mustard Quickly

In the game of Clue (Cluedo in the U.K.), players race their pieces around the board to be the first to discover who did what, where. Being fast helps. Quick thinking, asking the right questions first, and speedily traversing the game board with larger rolls of the dice all help.

Because mispricings can be short-lived, the stock market is a similar game. Scads of other investors are scouring the planet for unexploited opportunity. The winner will be the person who figures out the problem first, and there is no consolation prize for being last. So speed matters.

In an effort to get faster, you should remove the parts of your process that add no direct value. Frictional busywork can be found in many places. The mandatory spreadsheet, the multi-page investment hypothesis, and the rigid pre-scheduled committee meeting are all drags on success. Companies of all sizes have these and other inefficiencies, but they are frequently pathologies of larger investment management firms. I once knew a firm that held idea evaluation meetings (nicknamed "Pitch and Bitch") at a fixed time on alternating Tuesdays. Apparently you were required to spend the other 339 days of the year waiting.

Accelerate your process by using a divide-and-conquer strategy. Split the job into three parts — Insight, Approval, and Trade — and work to reduce the duration of each.

First, reduce your "Time to Insight" by allocating time to your most productive activity. This is different for different investors. Screening? Model-driven sensitivity analysis? Chats with management? Wherever your edge comes from, make sure you are spending most of your time doing it. Know that the 80/20 rule applies here: 80% of your insight comes from the first 20% of your research. Your goal should be to move toward a conclusion as fast as prudently possible.

Next, reduce "Insight to Approval", the period where you know you have an investable opportunity but it needs to clear other hurdles. This step can become cumbersome if a large number of people are involved. Unfortunately the activities of stock picking and describing a stock pick are two separate skills. In the worst-case scenario, an investment approval committee looms. These groups oftentimes require Oscar-worthy performances and Churchillian political maneuvering to overcome the objections of the politburo. If you're in such an environment, accelerating the execution of your ideas probably involves improving your interpersonal and presentation skills. Going to charm school and dance class won't necessarily improve your investing, but especially if you are at a large firm, these skills will ultimately help you move faster.

Finally, now that you have a great idea and it has been approved and put in context with other portfolio holdings, it's time to reduce "Approval to Trade", that dead-air space between when you know what you are going to do and the moment when you actually do it. Operational and compliance factions often control this part of the process. Are these important concerns? Yes. But from an investment perspective, value is only lost during this period.

One more thing. While you are at it, make sure you have fast systems. Occupational-studies experts estimate that the average person clicks their computer mouse between 400 and 3,000 times per day. If you are at the low end of the range, say 1,000 clicks/day, an extra half second of latency per click will cost you more than 50 hours every year, or more than a full week of work!

Speed is your friend. When your process is perfected it should look like a Formula One pit stop: smooth, efficient, and snappy. Just like a Grand Prix pit crew, break this complex task down into its component parts. Don't waste conversation. Be ready to handle contingencies. And do it all in as short a time as possible, because other crews are racing to beat you.

30. Higher

Stock-picking fulfills every marketer's ad slogan. It is the gift that keeps on giving. No, there is no finish line. And yes, you must think different. But perhaps the most applicable tag line is Target's: "Expect more. Pay less."

It is no accident that some of these most memorable slogans capture the open-ended creative landscape of investing. Just like some of the most desirable products, the promise is one of opportunity, challenge, and perpetuation.

If investing were a sport, it would be the pole vault. Imagine the exhilaration when you successfully clear the bar, landing on the mat looking up at what you have just achieved. However, even before the crowd's cheers recede, a thought slips in: There is another height. A height you can't clear today. And thus this sport, this endeavor, always ends in failure. There is always a height you cannot clear. But you are going to try anyway. And over time, for the trying, you will end up going higher than you otherwise would have. This is the nature of pole-vaulting.

It is also the nature of investing. It is both a curse and blessing of the profession that you can produce a level of return today, but with diligence, education, effort, speed, training, evaluation, thrift and discipline, you can in fact produce higher returns tomorrow. This improvement is unbounded. You can always move the bar higher, and there will always be a level of return which you cannot achieve today. The gift that keeps on giving indeed...

It doesn't matter if you are a weekend investor or a billionaire fund manager. The aim of your next investment effort is identical. Go higher.

31. Channel Scooby-Doo

Being a good stock picker is like being a detective in a murder mystery. You piece together clues in hopes of solving a puzzle. As you move from story to story, you will realize that no two plot lines are exactly the same. And yet you can develop techniques that will crack the case more often than not. It just so happens that there is a lot to learn from famous gumshoes as you solve *The Case Of The Company And The Price That Doesn't Match.* Consider borrowing tools from the greats.

Sherlock Holmes approaches cases with a blank mind, doesn't "twist facts to suit theories but rather lets the theory twist to suit the facts" and believes that "once you eliminate the impossible, whatever remains, no matter how improbable, must be the truth." He is also a data freak who warned against reasoning with insufficient information, once exclaiming, "I can't make bricks without clay!"

Francophone Hercule Poirot doesn't waste much time with the physical evidence but instead believes that, by talking with people involved, the answer will be revealed through their lies or their truths. He simply employs "the little grey cells" and a fastidious O.C.D.-like commitment to his process, which he repeatedly refers to as "order and method." (The books on his shelf are arranged according to height.) Also, despite being perfectly fluent in English, one of his favorite techniques is to feign misunderstanding in order to milk more information from his target.

Quincy (and many of his CSI-derivative cousins) uses a scarce and specialized knowledge base (in his case, medicine) to see things that other investigators miss.

Miss Marple believes that human nature is constant. She only has look at how someone in her small village of St. Mary Mead will act and she will be able to correctly divine the choices that other less savory characters have made.

Columbo uses a two-step process, first getting his target talking using meaningless banter and seemingly innocuous inquiries, then surreptitiously inserting the real question into the flow of conversation. His targets' verbal momentum is simply too great, and by the time their thinking catches up with their words, it is too late.

Nancy Drew, the Hardy Boys, and the Famous Five are all consistently underestimated because of their youth and their position as outsiders. They are simply never perceived as a threat, and they sneak up on solutions undetected.

Joe Friday famously wants "just the facts", and his process is one of raw hard work in data-gathering, removal of confounding nonsense, and distillation of the remainder until nothing is left but truth.

Phillip Marlowe drinks whisky and smokes Camels. (Consider using these techniques sparingly.)

Like detectives, professional investors have their own methods for solving the market's mysteries. Some have been known to go so far up the supply chain that they ask packaging firms about order patterns for a specific retailer's bags. Peter Lynch famously used to monitor how many cars were in a company's parking lot. Steven A. Cohen went to industry experts who were familiar (perhaps too familiar, it ends up) with current trends.

Opportunities for clever market sleuthing are continually evolving. Satellite imagery now allows investors to infer agricultural conditions, coal stores at utilities, and inventory at automakers. Also, many now use Internet-search trend data to determine the social-media velocity of a product. The tools you use to solve your specific cases are limited only by your knowledge of the playbook and your creativity. At this point, please re-read chapter 26.

Regardless, whether you focus on real or fictional investigators, there is a lot to be gained from emulating the masters. Elementary, my dear Watson!

32. It's Not A Job, It's A Lifestyle

Finding undervalued securities is more of an obsession than a profession. The moment a news headline flashes across the screen, I see ticker symbols. The longs come first: immediate beneficiaries, then lateral ones. After those come shorts. I can't help it; at this stage it's just reflex.

In the supermarket, at the sidelines of my kid's soccer game, at the movies, in the shower, while waiting in line at the Department of Motor Vehicles and, I am ashamed to say, when hearing news stories involving horrible human tragedy. The ideas come. Here's a bold forecast: If you are good at this, it will become tiresome to the loved ones who surround you.

The writer David Foster Wallace once told this joke:

"There are these two young fish swimming along, and they happen to meet an older fish swimming the other way, who nods at them and says, 'Morning boys, how's the water?' And the two young fish swim on for a bit, and then eventually one of them looks over at the other and goes, 'What the hell is water?'"

It takes full immersion to succeed in this business. If you don't absolutely love this, so much so that you don't even know you are doing it, quit now.

33. Find Change

In Ray Bradbury's short story "A Sound of Thunder", a time travel technology has been developed allowing tourists to go back in time to see dinosaurs. Special precautions are taken so that nothing in history is disturbed, but one frightened customer strays off the path and inadvertently treads on a single butterfly, killing it. All is well until he returns to the present day only to discover that his misstep has diverted the course of history. Words are now spelled differently and the outcome of a presidential election has been reversed.

Today, every single change you see is a crushed butterfly giving birth to a chain of subsequent events — a new and different future history. Sometimes these changes are incorporated into share prices very quickly. Sometimes they aren't.

Different future histories create different cash flows, and what is a stock price other than the sum of a company's discounted future cash flows? If you can figure out a changing cash flow stream faster or more accurately than the average investor, you can find a mispricing.

What is changing right now? What changes are accelerating or slowing? Who benefits? Who loses? And most important: of the answers to all of these questions, which have not been priced in yet by the stock market?

Forecast the path of a change as it moves forward in time. Perhaps the protagonist from the movie *Gladiator*, Maximus Decimus Meridius, said it best: "What we do in life echoes in eternity."

34. The Antidote To Anecdotes

One illusion in investing's hall of mirrors is the chimera of anecdotal observation. This is the insight delivered by a single, vivid and often personal experience. These insights are deeply imprinted — so deeply that we tend to overlook that they're a single anecdote...one of hundreds of thousands or even millions of different data points. Our singular experience is perhaps something to investigate further. However, alone it means nothing. The problem is, it doesn't *feel* that way.

Newer analysts are particularly susceptible to this trap. Perhaps their daughter has purchased a new, unfamiliar brand of shoes, and "everyone at school is wearing them." This information then becomes part of the investment mosaic. Too much a part of it. Despite the fact that your analyst's daughter is in only one of the many fashion cliques in her school, that her school is one of tens of thousands in the country and that she is only one of tens of millions of female students nationally, 48 hours later you are listening to the analyst hyperventilate the plan for Zippiez Shooz overthrow of Nike on its way to eventual global domination.

Anecdotes have a powerful and disproportionate impact on our thinking. They are a part of a larger perceptual distortion that we all often fall victim to, which is that we tend to overweight marginally significant information that is known, even though larger unknown variables are the dominant ones. Have a bad experience at a publicly listed restaurant? I challenge you to keep that event from stealing into your subconscious the next time you look at the company's stock.

Knowing something with certainty, even when nobody else does, doesn't make it a more important piece of information. Something can be known or unknown, important or unimportant. These are two independent characteristics. Think of them like milk and beer. Both are good, but you don't want to mix them up.

35. Anecdotally...

It's worth noting that the informational value of some anecdotes is changing. In the U.S., you can see it on a national scale as regional differences fade and blend. Less frequently do you hear an accent from Bangor, or Fargo, or Fayetteville. Coastal trends seem to move inland just after the HTML photons describing them travel down the fiber-optic cable. More than ever before, we are one people. Of course this is occurring on a global basis too, which helps explain why a Korean pop star singing unintelligible lyrics can elicit more than a billion global YouTube views.

The power of an anecdote is subject to "tipping point"-style analysis. Networking effects driven by social media can accelerate new trends in a nonlinear fashion. Some snowballs stop. Some roll downhill. Some become avalanches.

In general, avoid using anecdotal observations in your investment decision-making. This skeptical stance will more often than not serve you well. But if you hear a rumbling, look back over your shoulder just in case there's a mountain of snow coming at you fast.

36. Avoid Cults Of Geography

The investors of any town tend to have unusually large stakes in home companies. St. Louis, Redmond, and Bentonville have high concentrations of ownership in Monsanto, Microsoft, and Walmart respectively. Approximately 15% of all outstanding Coke shares are held by residents of Georgia, most from Atlanta. Sometimes company towns even remain company shareholders long after the firm has downsized or departed. The residents of Schenectady still love their GE.

Unfortunately, familiarity breeds complacency. Positions grow too large. Risks are overlooked. Missteps are too easily forgiven. Just like you make allowances for your rude old friend when he curses too loudly, blows his nose on his tie, and scratches his nether parts in public (let's face it, he might not be your friend if you were to meet him for the first time today), hometown investors always seem to forgive a local company even when it's not deserved.

A declining stock is particularly dangerous. Because of the longevity and historical stability of a marquee firm, locals underweight bad news and are mystified by lower share prices, often mistaking them for opportunity. "Mother Kodak is trading below $40, so it must be a buy." Ask the population of Rochester, N.Y., how that trade worked out.

Similar outcomes befell Enron's fans in Houston, Montgomery Ward's in Chicago, Polaroid's in Cambridge, and WorldCom's in Hattiesburg, Mississippi. Avoid investing in local companies.

37. Give Yourself Time To Digest

Any time you boot up the Internet to do research, you are trying to drink from a fire hose. The volume of information available is broad, deep, of varying relevance, and potentially overwhelming.

But there is a hierarchy of importance — some bits are smaller, shorter-term hors d'oeuvres of information. Skip these if you wish. Others are the biggies; they have a large and long-lasting impact. Get these wrong and it won't matter how many of the others you get right: it will be very difficult for you to outperform. Unfortunately, the Web doesn't differentiate one type of information from the other. And to complicate matters further, these relevant bits are floating in an ocean of irrelevant pseudo-information. When you're drinking from the fire hose, you get the whole goulash.

How to separate the important chunks from the rest? It is said that a very intoxicated Winston Churchill was once confronted by Bessie Braddock, a prominent, but homely, politician of the era. Shocked, she exclaimed "Lord Churchill, you are drunk!"

Churchill replied "And you, Bessie, are ugly. But I shall be sober in the morning."

What is important? Things that are distinct. Observable. Permanent.

Equally important is taking the time too spot these things. Our minds work like a traffic intersection. The light turns green and as information passes through, we process it. Then the light changes and we process a different thought from a different direction. This all works well until we try to make decisions more rapidly. As the lights change more quickly, smaller and smaller amounts pass through the junction each time. At the extreme, the lights change so quickly that nothing gets through the intersection at all. You are frozen, not processing, achieving nothing.

The challenge is to meter the amount of information you're trying to process, and simultaneously separate the informational grain from the chaff. The easiest way do this is to take a moment to digest the information you have gathered. Having time to think is just as important as having information itself.

So indulge in a thoughtful pause. It could last a minute or a day. Turn away from the screen. Stare out the window. Breathe.

Now sort the informational ingredients. Which are most important? Which will affect company financials the most? Which will dominate investor thoughts? Focus on these; return to the rest later.

38. Seek Asymmetry

As you read this, there is a set of stocks lurking in the stock market right now with better than 50/50 odds. They are asymmetric: the chance and magnitude of an increase in price is greater than the chance and size of a decline. Recognizing this setup, and allocating capital in proportion to the opportunity, are the most important skills you can have in this business.

This is so important I am going to repeat it: Recognizing a 60/40 proposition and investing accordingly is what you need to be successful in this business. That is *all*.

Half of this probabilistic tilt comes from a characteristic of the company which prevents its share price from a steep drop. Different investors call this different things. Backstop. Margin of safety. Upside/downside ratio. (See chapter 78.)

Regardless of what you call it, begin with the balance sheet. From it you can derive the worst-case scenario, floor, melt-value of a firm. Compare this figure to today's share price. When these two numbers match, you have the birth of a margin of safety — that magical zone where it is more difficult for a stock to go down than to go up. If the share price is anywhere near your calculated figure, you are probably onto something.

The other half of an asymmetric distribution is the sunny side. What can happen if things go right? This is the optimistic Tomorrowland that the majority of investors focus on when they look at a stock, and it is the meat of most investment websites, newsletters and blogs. To get the full advantage of asymmetry, it is important that you get to this hypothesis early, before it is priced by all investors.

Look for asymmetric distributions. Where the friction of downside protection has skewed future outcomes. Where twin tailwinds of improving fundamentals and improving sentiment have bent the odds your way. Where the playing field is tilted downhill.

The idea is to change this from a gamble to a profession, because gambling is a different proposition altogether, and should be avoided. As Elbert Hubbard once observed, "The only man who makes money following the races is one who does it with a broom and shovel."

39. Read Broadly

Mosaic theory, the idea that an investment hypothesis is born from an array of disparate informational wellsprings, suggests that people with a broad knowledge base have an advantage. The best way to get this foundation is through reading.

Reading can be a real chore for investment researchers. It is essentially what we are doing most of the day anyway, so the thought of cracking a book in your free time can be unappealing. But we all need as much of an edge as we can get, and broader perspective can be an actionable advantage. As Will Rogers observed: "There are three kinds of men. The one learns by reading. The few who learn by observation. The rest of them have to pee on the fence for themselves." He was talking about electric fences.

Most in this profession seem to lean toward nonfiction for their free-time reading. Biographies can teach you how the great outliers of the human race think and solve problems. Books about events let you enter a different moment in time, draw analogies to today, and help you forecast what might happen next. Books that survey a phenomena through time (automobiles, interest rates, navigation, baseball, horticulture...the list is infinite) reveal the keys to process, advancement and improvement.

Fiction won't kill you either. Reading fiction gives you the ability to walk around in someone else's shoes for a while...to become someone else with different emotions, desires, perceptions, biases, and motivations. The ability to see the world through others' eyes is important in investing. After all, some of the questions you must answer are: Who will be the next buyer of your stock, at what price, and why? What is that next buyer looking for? What does she see? How does she feel?

Of course you are reading a book right now, so some of this encouragement to read is wasted because you are obviously in the club already. Next time, however, consider reading something that is not about investing. Something wildly different. Something that expands your peripheral vision.

40. Avoid The Reality Distortion Zone

C-level executives traverse planet Earth surrounded by a force field, as if they were some sort of capitalist superheroes. Within this zone, everything is good, the sun is always shining, and honey flows from the faucets. Beware.

Upper-level management did not ascend to the pinnacle of their organizations by being unconvincing communicators. No, these are the survivors of a Darwinian battle of ascendency, with the winners determined by who is best at expressing an idea. Not only do they have the best delivery, but they also have the best raw material. They are not saying anything that hasn't been vetted, rehearsed, and tested. That anecdote that proves the business case? The punch line has been tuned over the course of hundreds and hundreds of prior tellings.

A woman I know who idolized a certain New Jersey rock star was very excited to learn that he would be touring in Australia while she was living there. She bought tickets for both Sydney shows, on consecutive nights. In the middle of the first night's show, completely impromptu, the rocker interrupted the entire concert, sat on the edge of the stage, and fought back the emotion as he told a revealing personal story about his youth. You can probably guess what happened the next night...same interruption, same tear-jerking story. His voice even hitched at the same point in the monologue. It was a show. And so is the story that the company's CEO just told you.

I am always mystified by those who choose to attend the Berkshire Hathaway annual meeting in Omaha. Here, tens of thousand of people gather in a stadium and for hours watch a very articulate management team answer questions on stage. Their images are projected on a huge Jumbotron just like rock stars. Attendees even get candy and ice cream! It's a financial love-in.

This is not really an annual meeting but an evangelical sermon delivered to the faithful. They are probably a fantastic management team and company— but after attending, you will have lost your ability to tell. Somewhere between tapping your foot to the ukulele and that last bite of the Blizzard, you've lost all objectivity. If you ever come to a moment when the correct decision would be to sell the stock, you will hesitate (and lose more money than you should).

A management's siren call is not the only problem. Corporate operations can often be overwhelmingly impressive to the point that they dilute your critical abilities. I once toured a plate-manufacturing plant in Corning, N.Y. It was a circuitous tangle of pulleys and spinning wheels with suction cups all connected by belts, leading to an alternating application of fire, water, and molten glass. At the far end, a stream of perfect dinnerware exited. It was as if Rube Goldberg hired the creator of the game "Mousetrap!" to build a manufacturing facility, with Salvador

Dali consulting. It was the most incredible feat of engineering I had ever seen.

Within just a few years, however, that very same facility was subsequently sold, and plate production was largely off-shored. It simply wasn't profitable.

Light bulb — it didn't matter how gobsmacked I was with the facility. I was in no position to judge its economic viability.

And so it is with most every business. Can you really tell a good pharmaceutical research lab from a bad one? A trading floor? A paper mill? Be honest.

Undertake defensive measures to sterilize your contact with companies. Focus on meetings off-site, away from the reality-distortion zone. When possible, attend industry conferences rather than making individual company visits. This way, when framed next to a baseline of other industry participants, it will be easier to tell if a company is truly something special.

Also, while you're at these conferences, don't just focus on the companies. Look at the other investors, your peers. In no other endeavor will you find a more insightful band of cynics and professional critics. They know a lot about your target company and will probably be willing to chat for a moment. Ask open-ended questions like, "Have you met this management team before?" or "Did you hear anything new today?" Be ready for an earful.

41. Beware Of Greeks (And All Other Nationalities) Bearing Gifts

Around Christmastime in 1974, Phillip Kunz, a sociologist from Provo, Utah, sent out almost 600 Christmas cards. These cards were normal in every way, but for one fact: they were sent to complete strangers in Chicago. Amazingly, not only did Kunz receive a wave of replies, but some included handwritten notes, three-page family updates, and photos of weddings, graduations, and children. Fifteen years later, Kunz was still receiving Christmas cards from some of these strangers! Why?

Deep within our social DNA is an obligation to return favors which have been kindly given to us. Sociologists believe that this behavior is taught in all global societies without exception. As a species, we have observed, that giving is not just about sacrifice and loss but rather a mechanism which can protect, diversify, and expand our path through life. Giving back makes us both individually and collectively stronger.

Not everyone uses this social rule for altruistic purposes, and it is not lost on profit seekers that we have all been conditioned from a very early age to reciprocate others' generosity. You don't have to look far to see them using your years of social training against you. It's why waiters leave mints on the tip tray, condo salespeople give you a free night's stay, and the American (fill in the blank) Society sends you address labels with its solicitation letter.

Our business is no exception. In meetings with management teams, there are often little tchotchkes which apparate during the conversation. Perhaps a T-shirt, a toy for your children, or a logoed cap. Or even something unique. Over the years I have been offered a woman's handbag, Knicks tickets, live lobsters, a dartboard, an assortment of couture cheeses, popcorn and chocolate-covered cherries, a football helmet with my name on it, and a Mr. Potato Head kit. Were these really gifts, or baited hooks?

There are three ways to inoculate yourself from the reflex of undeserved reciprocation. The first is the easiest: don't accept. Pretend these gifts are radioactive. This leaves you clean. Socially unburdened. Untouchable. Walmart, a company that knows a thing or two about buyer psychology, in its *Statement of Ethics* simply forbids employees to accept any gift for any reason.

Second, recognize that the "gift" you have in your hand is nothing of the sort. It is really a payment and wasn't born of kindness or affection but instead is simply an advance on your compliance. An uninvited advance. You owe the "giver" nothing — they broke the social protocol first by twisting a social convention for personal gain.

Another way to absolve your obligation is to re-gift quickly, before the radioactivity rubs off. It's not really yours if you pass it on quickly to someone in need, right? Surely there is someone else in the office who could use a Mr. Potato Head.

42. Listen To The Yin And The Yang

The bond market and stock market are two opposing and balancing, symbiotic pricing mechanisms. Each has its strengths and flaws.

The bond market is a bigger, smarter, stronger critic. It is an X-ray machine that sees the skeleton of a firm and measures its health. If it were a person, the bond market would be a bald guy with shirtsleeves rolled up, hairy forearms bigger than your neck, tie pulled down, and sweat stains under his arms. If you're a company, don't lie to him. He'll detect it and kill you. By the way, he hates cash outflows such as new business initiatives, dividends, and share repurchases. You do too much of this sissy crap and he's going to make you hurt.

The equity market is a forward-looking probability-and-payoff confabulation machine. It prices the imbedded call option within a business — the patent, the well-bore results, the upcoming FDA trial, the smaller and more rapidly growing product line that just might work out. The equity market is a hopeful opportunist with nice clothes that don't look good on him because he got dressed too quickly. He's a young, talkative, glass-half-full type.

He's a little hunched because he always sits forward in his seat. He sometimes walks into an oncoming car because he is looking at the sky. He is deathly afraid of the bond guy.

Some investors believe that movement in the bond market precedes movement in corresponding equities. I know two portfolio managers who use this phenomenon as the core of their investment process. They are very successful and often have a thoughtful, I-know-something-you-don't-know look about them. When grilled, this is how they describe the world:

> Moves in the bond market lead the equity market by about six months, give or take. This is because fixed-income vigilantes are focused on the balance sheet, and it is here where subtle changes occur first. These changes, and corresponding shifts in spreads, can happen before there is any detectable effect on the income statement. When receivables slip from 40 to 48 days, when inventories change disproportionately, when debt loads swell or shrink, or when other debits and credits stutter, fixed-income investors re-price the debt. Equity investors, not.

These spread trends are often best observed on an industry basis first, after which you can drill down to the stock-specific level. Also, the high-yield market is the best place to start: more spread means more variability and easier detection of changes. (In contrast the credit default swap market — or what's left of it — is more noisy, undependable, and just plain manipulated. Compare this to the high-yield market, where investors are committing real capital — in many cases buying large slices of an entire issue of debt.)

The big, bald, mean bond guy is really your friend. Trust him, and he will not only keep you out of trouble but also show you improving situations — before anyone else.

43. Find The Rhythm

The stock market (and industries within it) wax and wane in seasonal, cyclical, and long-wave patterns. There is no exact, xerographic repetition, but there is a resonance. Like a surfer waiting in the line up, watching the waves: no two are the same, but they keep coming.

Beyond the waves themselves are the sets of larger and smaller groups of swell. Even beyond that are the high- and low-pressure systems which give birth to storm surges. And so on. Yes, there is some randomness within the Russian-doll layers of patterns, but patterns they are.

Mark Twain is said to have put it this way: "History does not repeat itself, but it often rhymes." Don't make the mistake of committing to a repetition of exact events. Instead, bet heavily on the rhyme.

Within my own career, there has been ample time to observe some of the short-cycle patterns. The seasonal ones are easy to spot. An older executive in the energy industry told me to buy the natural gas stocks when you see geese flying south, and sell them when you see your first daffodil bloom. He hasn't been that far wrong. The CEO of a ski resort company said that his stock always goes up when it snows in Central Park. The retail industry, and sentiment surrounding it, are notoriously seasonal.

Beyond seasonality, longer industry cycles can also be spotted. Like a familiar Hollywood plot line, the story is structurally identical, but the surrounding details vary. Industry gets profits, industry loses profits, industry gets profits back.

This story of strong industry profits born of high levels of capacity utilization, followed by margin-destroying over-expansion, is a dependable one. When times are good ebullient, overconfident management teams over-invest as they straight-line their business forecast up and to the right. With all industry participants behaving similarly, the seeds are planted for the cycle's decline.

Soon enough, too much supply finds itself chasing too few customers, profits atrophy, and before long the industry in aggregate is losing money. Weaker, over-leveraged players go bankrupt, and their capacity either disappears or is absorbed into the limping survivors. From these ashes a new industry structure rises, with fewer participants, more bargaining power, hardened management, lean cost structures, and higher operating leverage. The cycle is now ready to begin anew.

This pattern recurs in industry after industry. Look at any cycle: housing, semiconductors, autos, steel, chemicals, agriculture, mining, skilled labor...ad infinitum. All repeat. All are cyclical. All are mispriced at certain points in the cycle.

Other phenomena lurk beyond industry cycles. Like a big flywheel slowly spinning, I think I can also see a larger, long-wave pattern. When I entered this business, the old guard was populated with hard, thrifty, critical, numbers-centric analysts. They were students of financial statements and had little time for growth narratives. I now see that they were simply born of difficult times. They lived the death of equities, inflation in the teens (and mortgage rates of 17%!), and a fracturing of the U.S social structure during the 1960s. These were the survivors — the sharks and cockroaches who survived the nuclear winter that desiccated the equity industry for nearly three decades. They were the best at what they did. Yet all of them without exception were left completely disoriented by the tech bubble of 1997 to 2000. After the disbelief and anger stages passed, they simply walked around the office like zombies. Many quit. Those that remained never really regained their life force, their taste for the industry.

My point is that the pattern seems to be starting up again. Like perceiving the curvature of the Earth as you climb to altitude, things just might be circling around. The young analysts in our office sound like the old guard I remember. They are hard. They feel lucky to have a job (most of their friends really don't.) Their analytical glass is half empty. They have never known a period of extended euphoria. Put them in a way-back machine and they would fit in, exactly, with my mentors from the old days. The cycle repeats.

44. We Do Not Live In Unique Times

Every time today's market pundits describe the concern *du jour* as "unprecedented," they reveal a shortsightedness that impairs their credibility. Read *Reminiscences of a Stock Operator,* by Edwin Lefevre, or Benjamin Roth's daily entries in his decades-spanning *The Great Depression: A Diary.* Then try and say that we are in some sort of uncharted territory. Change the names and dates in these books and they could be written today. When reading these accounts and many others like them, it becomes apparent that today's events are about as unprecedented as today's breakfast.

Think we are in an accelerating, unsettled world where the old rules don't apply? Or that our historic institutions are being threatened to the point where the future is becoming unstable? Are you disoriented by today's pace of change? Just be glad it isn't 1968.

The year began with the Beatles' Magical Mystery Tour at the top of the charts, and quickly slid downhill from there. North Korea captured the Naval Intelligence cruiser U.S.S. Pueblo and its crew. The North Vietnamese Army launched the Tet Offensive. Walter

Cronkite announced that the U.S. must negotiate a settlement to the Vietnam war. Minnesota senator/poet Gene McCarthy almost defeated incumbent Lyndon Baines Johnson in the Democratic primary after which LBJ announced that he would not run for president. And Reverend Martin Luther King was assassinated. All of this happened in 1968 — before May.

The rest of the year saw race riots sweep 100 cities across the United States, students occupy five buildings at Columbia University, students armed with shotguns take over the student union at Cornell, Valerie Solanas shoot Andy Warhol, Sirhan Sirhan assassinate Robert Kennedy, the Soviet Union invade Czechoslovakia, the Democratic National Convention descend into a riot, Nixon defeat Humphrey by a nation-splitting 43.4% to 42.7% popular vote, and the year finish with the youth of the nation celebrating "National Turn in Your Draft Card Day."

For those who lived through 1968, it must have seemed as if the fabric that held the world together was unraveling. Now compare that year with current events. Exactly what happening today is unprecedented?

For every event happening today and tomorrow, there is an historical analogue. Beware anyone who tells you that we are in historically bad (or good) times. This time is not different.

45. Small-Cap Snipers

Most larger firms are an amorphous mash-up. Each tends to be an overlapping gallimaufry of offsetting business lines, vertically integrated supply chains, disparate geographies, and assorted end-customer exposures. When researching these monoliths, it can be tough to find an actionable opportunity. As an investor, even if you do discover a misunderstood corner of the business, will it be big enough to move the needle?

It's different with smaller capitalization firms, where you can be very specific with your capital deployment, placing your chips on exactly the number you want. Most of these corporations have very narrow end-market exposures. If you discern a geography, industry or demographic group experiencing change, you are more likely to find a way to play it with a smaller company.

Do you want a Pennsylvania bank with seasoned management, high commercial loan exposure, and an overlap with Marcellus shale gas reservoirs? How about a semiconductor company with leverage to high-end European auto sales? Want a mortgage-servicing pure play? A red-state movie exhibitor? Pawn shops? Titanium dioxide? Organic milk? With smaller companies, you can take exactly the shot you are looking for.

As a student of the world's economic phenomena, you will unearth many opportunities. But oftentimes, smaller firms will offer the only path to monetize your insights. If your comparative advantage is based in microeconomics, the small-cap market is your playground.

46. Keep Your Weight Over Your Skates

In every team sport, there are many specialized positions. But there is always one where the player has to be ready to move quickly in any direction. Oftentimes this is the best athlete on the field.

Baseball's shortstop, rugby's wing forward, American football's defensive back, lacrosse's middie, cricket's wicket-keeper, basketball's guard, soccer's goalie. Pick your sport and you know the position. These are the players with their weight centered over their feet. They are 360-degree athletes, prepared to change course instantaneously as circumstances demand.

Intellectually speaking, these are the positions you want to mimic. Balanced, two-footed, centered and not committed to any specific movement. Able to assimilate new data immediately. Aware of subtle changes. Not married to any hypothesis. Inclined to reevaluate the scenario repeatedly and rapidly. Instructed by past events but not a prisoner of them. Ready to change your mind, and your direction.

47. Shift Your Schedule

What if, in advance, somebody told you a moment when your competition would be weaker and, moreover, that this moment would recur every week? Would you take advantage of it?

Well, this magical moment exists. It's called Monday morning.

Ever have a "case of the Mondays"? Well, that lethargic re-entry into the work week is not specific to you, or even the finance industry. You can see anecdotal evidence of Monday-itis everywhere. Ever notice heavier traffic, slower fast food orders, or an increase in your own vacant screen-staring? Urban legend says you should never have surgery on a Monday, lest you have the wrong limb amputated. There is even an academically documented day-of-the-week anomaly in the stock market which suggests that stocks decline between Friday's and Monday's close.

A significant percentage of my competition conducts Monday morning meetings, where analysts, portfolio managers, and strategists pretend they are not hung-over as they share clever-sounding, allegedly useful observations. I understand that this is an attempt to re-boot a new week, but if a vibrant exchange of ideas is the goal, a different morning would certainly work better.

Want to gain some advantage over the competition? Consider beginning your work week on Sunday. This not only eliminates the jarring Monday morning cold-start, but more importantly can be a quieter, more thoughtful time of the week when you can think strategically.

Monday isn't the only problem time. The end of the week holds similar difficulties. A recent study in the U.K. showed that people who had surgery on a Friday were 44% more likely to die than those who had a procedure earlier in the week.

So while you are rearranging your work schedule, why not just skip Friday afternoons also, especially during the summer? There is no liquidity. Everyone in the office is thinking about golf, their match.com date, little league, or the Kardashians. And after a long week of deep thought, the only decision that professional staff are capable of making is shaken or stirred. To quote a wise man who had 40 long years to consider human resources policy, "Let my people go!"

48. Focus On The Mass

The most important observation that value-investing patriarch Benjamin Graham ever made was this: "In the short term the stock market is a voting machine, but in the long run it is a weighing machine." His point was that popular opinion can fleetingly drive a company's share price in one direction or another, but in the end there is a deeper reality that doesn't vary with sentiment. And this reality defines what a company *is*.

Regardless of the tidal pull of positive or negative investor beliefs, there is an underlying, mathematical anchor which defines the value of a company. After accounting for measurement error, it's really not up for debate. This value is derived from tangibility of the balance sheet and the size and duration of the firm's future cash flows. The techniques for these calculations have been described in common finance textbooks for decades.

In your research you should first concentrate your focus on this, the mass of a company, because without this estimate you have no way of knowing if there is a mismatch between true value and today's share price. If you do the work and there is no mismatch, move along. There is nothing to be done.
However, if your work reveals a gap between value and price, trade: this is what you have been waiting for.

49. Practice Good Portfolio Hygiene

There is a graveyard within most investors' portfolios. These are the stocks — once young, fresh and beloved — that have now revealed their true character: half-swings, zombies, lies, hopes, fillers, jalopies, disabled, broken. It's not obvious that they are bad ideas, and they still have some endearing attributes such as a low valuation or the remnant promise of future success. But the reality is that they are hulks becalmed in an intellectual Sargasso sea. They are going nowhere.

If you hadn't purchased these stocks, you wouldn't own them today. Your historical relationship and better-than-average knowledge of the companies keeps you from pulling the chain, but pull the chain you should. At any given moment these stocks could represent a double-digit percentage of your portfolio, and removing this deadweight loss can have a dramatic impact on performance.

Review your portfolio on a fixed schedule, accounting for where your original investment hypothesis remains intact and where you've had "mission creep." For these latter stocks, test your conviction and show no mercy. Would you add to your position now? Are you excitedly anticipating the next data point to come from the company, or do you feel a nervous hope? Would you initiate a new position today? Be honest, cut and redeploy.

50. Use The Scientific Method

You will spend the most difficult moments of your career adrift and discouraged, snake-bitten by and idea which you realized, too late, was flawed.

Rather than seeing this as a single unfortunate event, think of it as part of an experiment. Gather it with your other stocks-gone-wrong, then like an art curator staring at an impressionist painting, step back. Do you see anything? Answer the question "Why?" This is the first step of the scientific method.

The structure of the scientific method sounds like long-winded shampooing instructions: form hypothesis, run experiment, analyze results, re-form hypothesis, repeat. But it provides a framework for learning from past events. Call it what you will: scientific method, continuous process improvement, kaizen, the school of hard knocks. This is how you get better. As Thomas J. Watson famously said, "If you want to succeed, double your failure rate."

It's not just about failure. In the framework of the scientific method, all individual outcomes, both good and bad, contain information. When linked, these events become like rungs on a ladder leading to investment enlightenment. Use them to get yourself to higher ground.

51. Quant Is Prelude

Quantitative analysis — applying math and statistics to financial data in an effort to pick stocks — is a good start. It is addressing the ball. Prologue. Foreplay. Appetizer. It is the intro, the warm-up, the preparation, the curtain-raiser.

It is a great beginning, not very unlike the great beginning of the great tale *A Christmas Carol* by Charles Dickens. The story starts with a visit from the ghost of Christmas past, who reminds us of what *has* happened. But when reviewing quant output, remember that the spirits of Christmas present and future have not spoken yet. Quantitative techniques look backwards only.

Yes, there are individuals who can use quant to extract excess return from the stock market. They work at firms that employ 250 hard-science PhDs, run computers that are digital Testarossas, and discuss the Higgs boson in their spare time. You are not one of them.

You can, however, use quantitative analysis as a preparatory step. Use rudimentary quant as an idea-generation tool, highlighting stocks which might be worth a closer look. Applied intelligently and diligently, this can tilt the probabilities ever so slightly in your favor at the very beginning of your process. After this, carry on with the rest of your modus operandi.

52. Ignore Taxes

More bad decisions are made because of taxes than because of tequila. As you contemplate a tax-related trade, there are two things going on which reduce the probability that you will make a good decision.

First, by avoiding taxes you are avoiding a cost, and it ends up that we are primordially wired to have a strong aversion to loss. This force is powerful, and some behavioral economists have estimated that we psychologically value the avoidance of a loss at twice the size of an equivalent gain. We simply get much more fulfillment out of not losing $100 than we do gaining $100. This becomes a problem when we undertake an action to minimize taxation, because we overvalue the benefit.

A second problem is that taxes, and the money that is saved through a tax trade, are mathematically certain. It just so happens that we value certainty too, and because of this, investors reliably overweight outcomes that are certain more than they weight outcomes that are probable. However, more tangible is not the same as more valuable.

For example, when given the choice, most people irrationally prefer to have $100 with certainty rather than a 90% chance at $125. This, despite the fact that when approached mathematically, the second offer is worth more — $112.50 — the expected value of all outcomes.

This phenomenon — a small certainty overwhelming the logic of a probabilistically uncertain outcome — is a risk of every tax trade. Combine this with the fact that you are avoiding a certain *cost*, and you might start making some bad decisions.

So don't trade (or postpone trades) for tax reasons. The psychological booby-traps are unavoidable and you will, on average, regret it.

Want an emotional salve? When it comes to taxes, try the Serenity Prayer, commonly used by Alcoholics Anonymous and other 12 step programs. It begins *"God, grant me the serenity to accept the things I cannot change,..."*

53. You Can't Time The Market

Despite having unrivaled access to the economic and political information of his age, John Maynard Keynes — the man who literally wrote the book on macroeconomics — entered the crash of 1929 with 83% of his assets in stocks. Oops.

Keynes was almost wiped out. After licking his wounds, he abandoned market-timing to focus on bottoms-up stock picking, concentrating on out-of-favor, dividend-paying value stocks. He subsequently had great results, and the returns from these later years cemented his reputation as not only a gifted economist but also an extraordinary investor.

The point of this story is that not even a genius armed with inside information can successfully execute a market-timing strategy. The challenges are many, including the difficulty of predicting future events of historically seismic proportion, behavioral demons which haunt the decision-making of all Homo sapiens, the short-time periods over which many abrupt market moves occur (particularly on the downside), and the reality that the market can stay irrational a lot longer than you can stay liquid.

The late Joseph Granville, the most renowned market timer of the 20th and early 21st century, had such power over markets that one day in 1981 he issued a call to "sell everything". The result was an immediate 2.4% decline in the Dow Jones Industrial Average on record volume. Yet when an independent firm analyzed his recommendations over the 25 years ending in 2005, it was revealed that he lost 20% on average. Annually.

I've often thought that, like the Nobel Peace Prize, the Darwin award should be split among multiple disciplines to recognize high levels of species-threatening stupidity in each area of human endeavor. Thus the Fen-Phen doctors could receive the award for medicine, Ted Kaczynski could take the literature prize, and the underground apothecaries who came up with bath salts would get chemistry. As for economics, market timers would certainly take home the gold medal.

Note that there are exactly zero market-timing mutual funds available today. Just like there are no Ouija board funds or divining rod funds or Beardstown Ladies funds. There is a reason for this: economic Darwinism. These methods simply don't work.

54. You Can't Time Sectors, Either

Another way to earn yourself a Darwin award in economics is to attempt to rotate capital among the various broad economic sectors. Most professionals use the 10 Global Industry Classification Standard ("GICS") sectors (Consumer Discretionary, Consumer Staples, Energy, Financials, Healthcare, Industrials, Information Technology, Materials, Telecommunications, and Utilities) to organize their investing. These are like 10 slots on a roulette wheel. You can bet on any one or any combination, or you can choose not to play.

In any given year, deviations between the performance of different sectors can be large — as large as the swings in individual stocks. So your decision to overweight the energy sector by 15% (because of your superior oil-price forecasting skills, or your ability to divine political events in the Middle East, or forecast GDP or weather or whatever other macro gift Mercury the god of commerce has bestowed upon you) — you should consider that move to be identical to buying a 15% position in a single stock. If you roll with position sizes that large, that's fine. Just make sure your customers are similarly aware, and that you wear your brown trousers to work every day.

Also don't forget that if you overweight one sector by 15%, you will, in relative terms, be short other sectors by the same amount. So forecasting that sector A will outperform is not enough; you will also need to correctly determine that sector B should be used as a source of funds in anticipation of its future underperformance.

When you analyze professional investor's portfolios, you will see active tilts in sector weights. However, when you talk to them, the sector weights are often being driven by something further down the stack at the industry or individual security level. There is a big difference between "My research indicates that investors don't fully understand Bluestar Pharma's FDA approval pipeline" and "I like the healthcare sector today." The former is a reasonable shot on goal. The latter is a roulette slot.

55. Exotic Geographies Are Great Places. For Vacations.

The excitement and promise of investing in a new and rapidly growing foreign economy can be very tempting. Beware these honey traps.

Your first problem is that you are probably not buying what you think you are buying. You're using road rules now. Whose revenue recognition standards are being used? What is an "independent" director? Where does the true ownership lie? What is the local definition of insider trading? Why does the state so often have a stake in the firm?

Most investors who own international stocks can't answer any of these questions.

Another issue with international investing is the currency mismatch. After changes in exchange rates are accounted for, nominal gains can evaporate. Also consider the balance between your personal financial obligations and financial assets. Are your liabilities denominated in Reales? Ringgit? Baht? Tenge? Hryvnia? Then why do you want your assets in these currencies?

Be especially wary of the latest way to separate frustrated domestic investors from their capital, "frontier" markets. I've been to Irian Jaya. Snuck into Burma. Travelled some of the " 'stan's." You. Will. Lose. All. Your. Money.

Obviously there is a spectrum of risk in investing in different overseas markets, but the most rational way to gain international exposure is to buy domestic companies with a large foreign presence. This way you can benefit from the demand trends, demographics, consumption patterns and comparative advantages of other geographies without having to endure the risks of local ownership.

In their search for growth, companies are increasingly looking to penetrate more and further into distant markets. This strategy used to be exclusive to larger firms (think soft drink companies and jet manufacturers) but as globalization has advanced, things have changed.

Today, every growth-hungry small and mid capitalization company also has an international strategy. Orlando, Florida-based Tupperware, for example, gets more than 65% of its sales from emerging markets, and analysts see this number eventually increasing to 80%. In Indonesia alone, the firm has 170,000 sales representatives who sell and distribute products to the country's 250 million people. As the archipelago's above-average G.D.P. growth drives ever more citizens into the middle class, Tupperware rides the wave. You can, too, as an investor in similar companies, and you don't have to endure many of the risks that come with headfirst investment into unfamiliar territory.

If you decide to ignore the above advice and instead invest directly into foreign markets, beware: some of your traditional risk-control techniques will not work. For starters, diversification won't save you on this one. Mashing up a group of flawed investments with broken incentives and offsetting currencies just leaves you with a bad batch of wombat stew. Furthermore, during times of market trouble, correlations between emerging markets increase. You thought you owned discrete assets on different continents, but exactly at the moment when you need diversification the most, it is revealed that you own only one thing. Risk.

56. Find A Forced, Involuntary Sale

Most of the time, price is the most important thing that an investor looks at when making an investment decision. But not always. Keep an eye open for involuntary, strategic, or otherwise value-insensitive participants.

Look for places where the execution of the trade is more important than the price: The Hart-Scott-Rodino mandated divestiture, the plan sponsor sloppily liquidating a former (fired) manager's holdings, the DOJ settlement disgorgement requirement, the painted-in-a-corner short squeeze, the larger-fund manager inadvertently caught in the low-volume Hotel California micro-cap ("You can check in any time you like, but you can never leave"), the public firm with new management boldly reshuffling its portfolio of businesses.

Within each of these is a forced, price-insensitive trade. They want a change, realignment, or solution. They don't want an amount — they want a goal.

You can help. Be a superhero. Enable the strategic! Rescue the litigated! Protect from the illiquid! Provide the solution to other's necessary needs and wants. You may be pleasantly surprised by the price.

57. Price The Exception

Sometimes cheap stocks aren't. They are actually being priced quite correctly. Watch out for these popsicle delusions — they look sweet and tasty, but what looks like an appetizing opportunity could soon melt away into nothing. In your valuation work, don't forget to discount for things like family control, illiquidity, dubious management, split class stock, opaque foreign ownership and undue influence of an off-center founder/CEO/chairman.

I've seen many ticker symbols scroll by that should have had an asterisk next to them. I will keep it vague to protect the quirky, but they have included the delusion-of-grandeur CEO who ran for president, dynastic media-family A-share control, nested and byzantine off-balance-sheet hideouts, cocaine-addled favored sons in the C-suite, side pocket compensation deals, CEOs with veritable harems, multiple alleged felons, and headquarters that made Versailles look like a nice country cottage. Once, early in my career, I left a management team at a strip club at 3 a.m. because I needed to get some sleep before their 8:30 a.m. presentation.

How much of a discount to apply? It is difficult to know exactly. But some of these structural impairments can be intractable and, ultimately, terminal. If you need a number, a *very* rough rule of thumb is 20%.

Why 20%? Well, why is the standard unit of doughnut purchases 12? Why does bad luck come in threes? Why does the itch start after seven years?

Just know that a discount of some number greater than zero needs to be applied, and 20-ish percent is the number the founders of corporate valuation agreed on some time during investment pre-history. Every situation is different. Start with -20 and customize accordingly.

58. Buy Growing Businesses

The stocks of Eastman Kodak, Montgomery Ward, and Polaroid each looked inexpensive many times during the decades they spent swirling around the bowl. From time to time, they may have even been temporarily mispriced — simply too cheap for the cash-flow stream that would leak out of the body during their corporate death throes. But it is important to recognize that the character of a shrinking company deteriorates daily, and with it declines your margin of safety.

This deterioration actually represents your best case, and ignores the self-inflicted wounds from the messiah manager the board just hired from the outside. You know, the one with a great track record from another industry who is going to cost-cut their way to prosperity, diversify into lateral-ish businesses, and spray money at consultants in hopes of curing a terminal condition. As if breathing in the vapors of a new Venn diagram will prevent people from taking pictures with their cell phones.

Why put yourself in a position where your backstop erodes every day? Growing businesses can be mispriced too. And as they increase and redeploy their cash flow, good things can happen.

They can repurchase shares and thereby reduce the denominator used to calculate a P/E ratio. They can pay a dividend, which in the U.S. implies a level of confidence in the stability and longevity of a company's profits. They can invest in new business initiatives, which can act like imbedded call options within a firm. They can even do that silly thing that the new outside CEO wants to do...but when it doesn't work for this company, it won't be fatal. Growth allows you to live another day.

Don't pick up cigarette butts on the sidewalk with a couple of puffs left in them. Don't buy wrapped-up slices of yesterday's pizza from the deli. Don't buy wasting assets. Don't go long atrophy. You know how the story ends — it's just a matter of when.

In contrast, there's no shortage of undeservedly inexpensive growing companies. Focus on these.

59. Don't Write It Down (Or Even Speak It) If You Don't Have To

Think for a moment about the words you would use to describe someone who makes a commitment and then sticks to it. Steadfast? Steady? True? Dependable? Solid?

Now switch it around. What words would you use to describe someone who changes his or her opinion suddenly? Fickle. Inconstant. Undependable. Wishy-washy. Flip-flopper.

Which of these would you rather be?

It is an inescapable truth that we live in a world where consistency of thought, speech, and action is valued, and we've all been trained from an early age to be true to our word. Unfortunately this behavior can dominate our actions even when circumstances change, steering us toward choices we wouldn't otherwise make.

During the Korean War, American prisoners of the Chinese were asked to describe how they felt about the United States. After prisoners told of the blessings of America, the captors would ask, "Surely there is something that is not perfect about your country?" With the reward of some rice or the possibility that family back home might be notified of their survival, prisoners would often identify some innocuous imperfection of the U.S.A. They would then be asked to write it down.

At the next meeting, it would be suggested that America wasn't really a great country. If the prisoner protested, it would be noted that it's certainly not perfect: "Look at this writing," the captors would say. "You said so yourself." And so the consistency trap was sprung. In this case, it was used in stepwise doses to gain increasing levels of compliance from captive U.S. servicemen. Eventually this included having them alert their captors to escape attempts, sing the praises of the communist system, and participate in radio broadcasts describing the evils of the United States of America.

In the stock market, circumstances change often. Do everything you can to prevent surrounding yourself with land mines of consistency. If you can help it, do not pitch a stock to multiple people. Do not repeat your hypothesis on a stock over and over again. Do not write down the reasons why your stock is going to go up. Do not publish or distribute your investment hypothesis on a stock. Do not go on record on the radio, TV, or in print in support of a stock. Do not tell your friends or family about a stock. Do not stand in front of hundreds of your peers at an investment conference and announce, as fund manager Bill Ackman recently did, that "this is not a trade for me. We're going to take this to the end of the Earth."

I'm not exactly sure where the Earth ends. But if it's longer than expected, Bill will run out of gas money before he gets there.

And with a commitment like that, he just locked himself in the car.

Consistency is an admirable personal attribute. It can also be a dangerous curse for an investor.

60. Be Careful What You Are Certain About

In 1997, a smart but erratic CEO with limited technical expertise returned to a computer company he had founded. He was rejoining the firm after having been fired unceremoniously in a very contentious, ugly and public manner. Now he was being brought back as a last resort.

The firm operated in a duopoly, but it was in trouble. Its market share had withered to less than 2% and was still shrinking. Floundering, the company was only able to survive via direct investment from its much larger competitor, which was eager to counter charges of anti-competitive behavior. Like a schoolyard bully caught *in flagrante delicto*, the larger company's claim to regulators could be summarized as "Look, we have not only taken our foot off of their throat — we are giving them oxygen!"

The consensus: Investors were *certain* the small company was irretrievably lost. Like so many other tech companies that had sputtered, this one too was headed for the technology graveyard. The math was grim. Sales in fiscal 1997 declined 28% year over year, the firm was losing over a billion dollars per annum, and the balance sheet was taking on water. Investor perceptions were even worse. Nobody believed that the new CEO, a quirky iconoclastic marketer with a history of working poorly with others, would be able to stop the company's free fall. The ghosts of Commodore, Data General, Digital Equipment, Tandy, and Atari were ready to welcome a new member to the tech hardware roadkill club.

Of course we are talking about Steve Jobs and Apple, and you know the rest of the story. Subsequent earnings growth, combined with an expanding multiple, led to a share price explosion. From Jobs' return to Apple until his death on October 5th, 2011, the stock increased 6,000%.

Most investors who looked at Apple in 1997 were certain, but wrong.

Certainties don't have to be about small things like companies. They can define our entire worldview. Right now you have bedrock preconceptions about how the world works. But consider these widely held certainties expressed prior to the most recent U.S. financial crisis:

- "The US housing market, in aggregate, has never declined."
- "The number of vehicles in operation in the United States has never dropped."
- "Demand for electricity in the United States cannot decline."

All wrong.

We all have preconceived certainties. But as Josh Billings said, "The trouble ain't what people don't know, it's what they know that ain't so." Some of our "knowledge" can be more dangerous than ignorance.

61. It's OK To Be An Atheist, But Pray Once In A While Just In Case

During your career you will encounter a variety of methods and perspectives that you think are raw bunk. They represent the different religious factions of investing. Maybe you think technical analysis, fundamentals, growth, value, momentum, small cap, large cap, behavioral analysis or fibonacci sequences don't make any sense. Maybe you would scatter chicken bones and blood on the floor before you would use one of these philosophies.

However, each of these cults has its own vote in the market. Other sects are moving capital based on their worldview, and therefore each has its own influence on supply and demand for a company's shares. Your disagreement with their ethos is irrelevant. It doesn't change their existence — or their impact on markets.

It's OK to wander into someone else's temple once in a while to meet their god. You might learn something, and at worst you will leave understanding better what drives your competitors' thinking.

62. Umwelt And The Umgebung

Alright, we are going to get a little New Age now, so light some incense and bear with me for a moment...

In the 1920s, an Estonian biologist named Jakob von Uexküll developed a theory about how organisms perceive their surroundings. He felt that each being experienced a limited and subjective subset of a broader reality, and each of these smaller realms of perception he called Umwelten.

An organism's Umwelt is its own personal bubble — an individually customized world of experiences. Everything the being perceives is included in its Umwelt, but anything beyond the edge of the bubble may as well not exist: it is simply excluded from the organism's consciousness.

Von Uexküll gave the example of a tick. Eyeless and deaf, the insect uses its skin's sensitivity to light to position itself high on a blade of grass, and its sense of smell to detect the odor of butyric acid (a marker which is secreted by the sebaceous glands of warm-blooded animals.) Using an organ specifically tuned to detect mammalian body temperature of 37 degrees Celsius (98.6 degrees Fahrenheit), the tick confirms that it has hit its target and weaves in between the hair follicles to attach itself to the skin.

This is the tick's Umwelt: light, butyric acid, temperature, hair and skin. That's pretty much it. You see how it is very unique, and different from say the Umwelt of a giraffe or a trout.

Taking the theory a step further, the aggregation of all Umwelts is called the Umgebung. This is the sum of all individual perceptions, motivations, experiences, and beliefs. The Umgebung is objective reality. The truth.

The only problem is that no individual can see it.

What does any of this have to do with investing? Look in the mirror. See who you are. You inhabit an uncommon and even unique bubble, don't you? Extrapolating your personal beliefs, perceptions, and economic decisions onto the populace at large is a dangerous leap. Ever wonder why stocks linked to NASCAR, pro wrestling, movie theaters, trailer parks, pawn shops, and virtually anything to do with the rural consumer can often be found at unnaturally low valuations? These industries are outside the Umwelt of the investing class.

The Umgebung is what sets stock prices, yet no individual can see it, including you. A first step to stock market enlightenment is self-awareness: Embrace the fundamental truth that you can only see your own Umwelt. Make allowances for the hierarchy of needs and decision-making of dramatically different investors, businesspeople, and consumers. Learn and respect your blind spots, and make efforts to grow your bubble. As you progress, you might just achieve investing Nirvana, where you become one with the Umgebung!

63. Avoid Wolf Packs

This was a tip I learned during my driver's education class when I was 17. When you're driving on an expressway, it's safer to avoid dense groups of vehicles going at identical, high speeds. The teacher called these "wolf packs."

In a wolf pack, you feel the comfort and confidence of a group, including the group's willingness to overlook established limits. Also, there is an inescapable social pressure to keep up or be left behind with the sloths you're overtaking. This is why speed limits on the thruway are often ignored. It's also how hyper-growth concept stocks get their grotesquely large valuation multiples.

The biggest wolf pack of my career was the internet bubble. At the beginning of it, all of us at my firm cockily laughed at neophyte investors paying high prices for such uncertain prospects. But by the end of it, after valuations had doubled and then doubled again, none of us were laughing. Our sober, time-tested style of investing was looking more and more like the mythical Polish cavalry charge, and our customers were increasingly coming to the conclusion that the world had changed — that we "just didn't get it."

At the peak I would ask our treasurer "How many today?" and she would mumble the number of clients who had fired us in the last 24 hours. Our firm was gradually slipping away. Choosing not to be in the pack had come with a cost.

The pressures to conform were so immense that they became existential. Individually we began to crack. One of us switched teams and funded an internet start up. Another preferred his office dim and quiet, Howard Hughes-style. One of us came in the office less frequently, and when he did walked around in a PTSD-like stupor. Several made other business plans, and left. Many of us began participating in unrelated pursuits: Politics. Building a hunting lodge. Ultra-marathoning. Others just drank.

Fortunately the laws of finance, mathematics, and common sense were only temporarily suspended, and the firm survived. But if the bubble had lasted another month or two we wouldn't have made it.

The worst-case outcome of wolf-pack driving is the multi-car pile-up. One driver falters — maybe the lead driver hits something, or maybe a weaker driver in the middle of the group wobbles — and the rest of the pack accordions into one another in an ugly chain-reaction. Running with the pack entails risks that don't always end well, and with investing it's the same. Outrageously popular stocks such as Microsoft, Cisco, and, more recently, Apple, don't usually lead to outperformance.

Yes, they are very comfortable to own. You will share a common experience with many other investors, and as the old wisdom goes, you will never get fired for owning IBM. But investing with the wolf pack won't produce excess returns, either.

At investment conferences I am always wary of the standing-room-only presentations sardined with eager analysts. This is where the wolf pack lives. I much prefer the room with the CEO in front, disappointedly staring at the empty chairs, beginning his presentation five minutes late after realizing that he is throwing a party that no one is coming to. Deflated, they always begin with the same milquetoast half-question: "Well, I guess we should start now..."

At most of these conferences the hosts also offer individual meetings with management teams. For more popular companies, getting these one-on-ones can be more difficult than finding a kidney donor. But I have a friend who does exactly the opposite — she schedules all her one-on-ones by waiting to the last minute, going to the conference desk, and asking for the least popular companies. Her first question to management: "So, why doesn't anyone want to talk with you?"

The reality is that successful investing is often lonely. The strongest practitioners think differently, are wracked with self doubt, and manically search for snippets of additional information. Their largest rewards come when one of their ideas graduates to popularity, but by then they are usually already harvesting their position and moving toward the next investment. Alone.

64. Narrative Trumps Quantitative

Stories are powerful mojo. They change people's minds. This is why lawyers use storytelling to persuade juries, why skilled salesmen talk about what a product does rather than what a product is, why politicians use jokes to make a point, and why good writers *show* you rather than tell you.

Even incorrect stories told well — think cold fusion, Martian canals, spontaneous generation, drowning by swimming less than one hour after eating, cell phones blowing up gas stations, you can keep your doctor — can persuade.

Stories can be so strong, in fact, that they can cause us to underweight or even ignore hard data sitting right in front of our eyes. This is because emotional and intellectual conclusions are two different things.

Emotionally anchored beliefs can overwhelm numerical evidence, and when they do, "I believe" trumps "two plus two equals five." Exhibit A: government lotteries. The odds of winning the New York State Lottery are 258,890,850 to 1. (You are 370 times more likely to be struck by lightning this year.) Yet all the people who play have bought into the story — the one that ends with them at the press conference, holding the oversize cardboard check.

In investing, stories are no less powerful. Narratives, unlike spreadsheets, trigger emotions. Even individual words such as "catalyst", "disintermediate", "duopoly" and "moat", when used to describe a stock, carry the ability to shift perceptions. The question changes from "How do I value this company?" to "How do I *feel* about this company?"

Part of this has to do with the nature of the numbers. The tangible, in-the-record-book numbers look backwards, whereas a story describes the future. And it is the future that the stock market is pricing.

Another part has to do with how we weight a narrative hypothesis. Stories drive perceptions, which in turn drive multiples. Because we overweight the narrative, oftentimes in spite of the data, we can end up with irrationally high (or low) valuation. Investors even have a name for these emotion-laden companies. They are called "story stocks."

This is how Krispy Creme Doughnuts stock got to a sugar-induced high of 375 times earnings in early 2004, or how British Petroleum spiraled down to four times after the Deepwater Horizon disaster in mid-2010. Within these irrationalities were mispricings waiting to be harvested.

When you shift from analysis to feelings, things can get dangerous. In aviation, there is a phenomenon where pilots navigating through zero-visibility conditions sometimes have distortions in their spatial awareness. Without sensory input, the inner ear begins to play tricks on the brain. The loss of equilibrium fools them into thinking that they are climbing, descending or changing course when actually they are not. (You may have had a similar experience while flying. Have you ever felt the plane is on a level course only to look out the window and realize you are actually in a steep turn?)

Sometimes pilots trust these feelings so much that they begin to rationalize why their instruments are wrong, and they make life-threatening "course corrections." Tragically, this is how John F. Kennedy, Jr., crashed his plane on a hazy evening in featureless, open water off Martha's Vineyard.

As you fly the friendly skies of the stock market, be conscious of your feelings, but don't let them overwhelm other, more rational inputs. Keep your eyes on your gauges, and believe them.

65. The Second Most Powerful Force In The Universe

It is said that when Albert Einstein was asked what the most powerful force in the universe was, he replied, "Compound interest."

The second on the list (though Einstein didn't say it) has to be the power of financial incentives. People do things for all kinds of reasons: power, passion, self-confirmation, revenge, fame — the list is long. But the one motivation that is observable, controllable, dependable, predictable, and remarkably underestimated is the power of money.

Financial incentives have been successfully used to get pregnant women to stop smoking, encourage children to attend school, induce college students to exercise, and get parents to pick up their children from daycare on time. In Israel, fertility rates have been linked to the cost of an additional child.

Litterers in New York treat their drinks differently based on even a tiny sum of money. Sixty percent of discarded bottles pulled from the Hudson River are from non-carbonated beverages despite the fact that they represent only 20-25% of all drinks sold. The difference? A five-cent refundable deposit for a container of anything with bubbles.

Recent legislation established a Securities and Exchange Commission Office of the Whistleblower, which offers a 10-30% share of any financial penalties imposed. Fraud tips, previously negligible, were recently counted at 6,500. Either thousands of people suddenly found their conscience, or financial incentives were at work.

If you pay people by the hour, they will maximize hours. (Know any lawyers?) Pay per job and they will maximize speed, lower cost and perhaps sacrifice quality. (Been to your doctor recently?) If you pay in advance, you risk becoming invisible. But if you pay in arrears, you will probably enjoy great service. (Applicable to plumbers, electricians, carpenters and other tradespeople.) The effect of these different incentive structures are as dependable as any law of physics.

Missing incentives are powerful too. When trying to explain why the Chicago Cubs have sucked for more than 100 years (last league championship: 1908), authors Jon Wertheim and Tobias Moskowitz note that the Cubs have the fifth most valuable Major League Baseball franchise, the third highest ticket prices (behind only the Yankees and the Red Sox), and enjoy the lowest attendance-sensitivity in the league. That is, of all the teams, Cubs attendance varies the least as wins or losses accumulate. The organization simply has less incentive to win because fans show up for the "Wrigley Field Experience" regardless.

For investors, shifts in a firm's financial incentives are particularly important because the implications are often not priced by the stock market at the time of the change. This is an important point. Understanding likely behavioral adjustments that will come in response to changing incentives can put you months ahead of the moment when the effect shows up on the income statement.

Recently I read a SEC filing from a data storage company. At the CEO's request, the board had altered his compensation package. He was now to be paid the minimum wage mandated by the state of California, and the rest of his compensation would be paid in company stock. It was an obscure filing, and the stock didn't do anything special that day. But just like Norse invaders burning their ships after landing, there is no retreat, no safety, no alternate strategy for this CEO — there will be success, or nothing. I will never have to wonder what his goals are, because he has only one.

On the short side, these incentive changes are just as important. I have seen several enterprise software firms self-immolate after altering their sales force incentives. It all looked great on the spreadsheet — raising minimums, capping bonuses, removing bonus accelerators. But at these firms, some of the most valuable assets are off balance sheet: they walk in and out of the door every day. Tamper with their incentives too much and they might choose to keep walking. This talent drain will lead to poor sales, which lead to poor earnings, which hurts the share price, which impairs management's financial incentives, and so on down the drain.

66. Remove All Frictions To Success

When Shakespeare's Hamlet said, "There's the rub", he may have been talking about suicide, or hard choices, or chafing. Regardless, he was definitely talking about some form of difficulty.

Without "the rub" getting in the way, his story would have made for boring theatre — but imagine how much further he would have gotten in life. This faster, more efficient Hamlet could have avenged his father's death in a quick and tidy manner, *and* he could have lived to tell about it. The play would have been a lot shorter, but that's the point here. The rub slows you down.

With stock picking, it's the same. This job is hard enough without the little frictions that restrict your freedom of thought. No single rub is a deal-breaker, but they compound in a sneaky, death-by-a-thousand-cuts fashion. All of a sudden, you realize you've just spent hours achieving absolutely nothing.

Every friction — the unnecessary meeting, the slow network, the redundant report, the extra password — is a cost. Accumulate enough of them and it can be as pleasant as walking through knee-deep mud.

What distractions slow your learning? What prevents you from thinking? From thinking *correctly*? From acting on your conclusions? From acting on your conclusions quickly?

Look at your investment process dispassionately, identify which of your daily activities are explicitly linked to finding mispriced securities, and cut away everything else.

67. Don't Ignore The Charts

Is there any actionable information in technical analysis—the study of a stock's past price movements? Why do investors calculate oddly chosen statistics from price data? Why would the value of a business, derived from expectations of its future cash flows, be related to the historical pattern of its shares? Why, at certain conspicuous price levels, are more shares of an issue suddenly offered to buy or sell?

One reason technical analysis matters is that in recent years, the barriers to entry have collapsed. Technical websites are abundant, and there has been a proliferation of related software, videos and tutorials.

The charts, and the rules of interpreting them, were once only available to the technical illuminati. At the beginning of my career, chartists would visit the office looking like archeologists with tubes of the Dead Sea Scrolls tucked under their arms. They would have cases of protractors and odd parallel rulers, and they would smell of stale cigarettes and accessorize with bifocals, suspenders, and ties that were too fat and too short.

Today this species is extinct; all of their craft is just a click away. Like an ascending spiral, technical analysis is experiencing a positive feedback loop. It is now more important because more people are using it, which in turn makes it more important.

Moreover it seems like there is something deeper within our evolutionary code which supports "the technicals." We are social, herding beings. We are also contemplative souls who look to past events as markers for future outcomes. And we are visual.

When my daughter was seven, she made a birthday card for me, which I have hanging in my office to this day. On it she drew a picture of a "good stock." It looked like this:

Technical analysts will recognize a stock breaking out of a basing pattern and shifting into a classic bullish channel, with higher highs and higher lows. If you overlaid moving-average traces on this chart, you would first see the slope of the 50-day moving average turn positive, then the 200, and in there somewhere you would see a time-honored bullish "golden cross" as the 50 d.m.a. overtook the 200. This is an archetypal chart.

When drawing a "good stock", why did a seven-year-old who knows nothing about the stock market draw the perfect trace — one which an old school technician friend used to call a "Picasso chart?"

Answer: because there are sociological truths installed within her, and within all of us, at a very young age. It becomes our intuition, reflex, and world view. Good = more = higher. Inescapable temporary setbacks occur, but can be overcome. Success leads to success. Getting to never before seen heights is an achievement.

These are the thoughts that are embedded in a seven-year-old's picture of "good."

Do technicals matter? Of course they do. Investors are deciding where to allocate capital based on the charts, so the charts are clearly affecting the demand for specific shares. And the cult is growing...

68. Technicals Aren't Enough

Technical analysis — "TA" — is an ingredient for investment success. But while it might be the sugar, it's not the whole cake. I've met dozens of technical analysts, from the squinting, graph-paper-and-suspender pioneers to the CNBC propagated icons of our era to the neo-technical whiz kids. Not one of them has ever touted their historical investment performance.

There are no physical laws — no Bernoulli's Equation, no Pythagorean Theorem, no Newton's laws — for share prices to obey. It is an ecosystem, and the desires of the organisms which inhabit it evolve and change. Sometimes they prefer growth or value or 200 dma's or stocks in the industry *du jour*. Changes in these preferences often occur suddenly, and that is a problem for technicians because the charts can be overwhelmed by shareholder Attention Deficit Disorder. Pretty pictures alone are not enough to hold investor capital.

Chart reading may work best in the short term, when a stock's trajectory is undisturbed by material events. During periods of informational drought, the chart *becomes* the data which investors weigh. But recognize that you are one press release away from a chartist horror show.

Technical analysis is one tool among many. Just like when you attempt to complete any other complex task, some assembly is required, and you will likely need more than one tool to complete the job.

69. The Place Where Technicals Work

Whether you are a smiles-are-good, frowns-are-bad amateur or you write your own pattern recognition and analysis code, there is a specific corner of the market where technical analysis is more likely to add value.

Recall that part of the hypothesis for the efficacy of TA is that we are herding beings. As more than one technical analyst has told me, "It works because it works." Group dynamics influence the share price. But in order to have a herding impact, you have to have a herd. So that means that you must focus your technical analysis on the busier corners of the market.

Look for orderly charts of well-populated companies with lots of eyeballs on the stock. Think companies with larger capitalizations, high daily volumes, and lots of analyst coverage. I once knew a technical analyst who calculated that there were 3 analysts for every stock on the NYSE, NASDAQ, and AMEX. His requirement, stated perhaps with a little hyperbole, was: "If I am doing TA, I want 15 analysts on each stock I look at!"

70. Chartist Beware

Beyond minimizing your use of technical analysis in illiquid, irregular, and under-followed companies, there are some situations where it makes sense to abandon the charts altogether. Stocks with a binary outcome are one example. Biotech comes to mind: particularly in today's environment, where material non-public information leakage has diminished, there is little opportunity for news to influence a stock, or for investors to begin to swarm on it, until public release. If the rat lives, the subsequent share price moves can be dramatic (and vice-versa.) However, investors know that the stock market police are watching. In a world of enhanced detection and more aggressive enforcement, charts reveal little before the event itself.

Another shortcoming of the technicals: charts are useless in mergers and acquisitions. Bidders are students of the financial statements. They see "TA" as an unintelligible and obscure language, like Sanskrit. In their minds, company bids are created via psychology, math, Excel and sensitivity analysis. To them, technical analysis is just cute witchcraft.

71. Your Critics Are A Gift

You may not have noticed it, but as you moved from grade school to your teen years and now into the professional realm, the volume of criticism you've had to endure has diminished. It's like a headwind lifting. Remember how in your youth, you couldn't get to the water fountain without hearing all about your stupid clothes, your big nose, and the peanut butter that's been stuck to your face since lunchtime? And later on, teachers would grade you frequently and mercilessly. If you played a sport, well, some of the coaches weren't the hugging type, were they?

Now fast-forward to today's professional you. Most of the time... nothing. There is no mechanism to deliver the tight feedback loop — from criticism to modification, then re-evaluation and back. It seems like you are lucky if you get some cryptic observations once a year during your performance review.

Maybe you are enjoying the lack of critical feedback. Who wouldn't? But don't kid yourself. The silence doesn't mean you are now perfect. It's just that fewer people are commenting on it. At least to you.

A cousin of mine who was describing the arc of her life once said, "I enjoyed my 30s because during them I really learned who I was." More likely, others learned who she was but didn't let her in on their conclusions. Thinking about it now, the confidence she felt probably was as much self-discovery as it was a shifting into the silent and rose-colored, critic-free zone.

Particularly in larger companies, there exists a weird vacuum blending sterile political correctness, a fear of litigation, and "appropriateness" (whatever that is). If you want proof that, as some religions believe, the human soul can be separated from the physical body, spend 10 minutes talking to your director of human resources. Newspeak isn't just a fantasy concept from a dystopian novel.

Within this wasteland, if you are lucky, there might be a person who one day breaks protocol to criticize you in some small way. Embrace it! That person has just given you a rare gift — one that can strengthen you. It might not feel pleasant to hear it, but when was the last time someone gave you a roadmap for improvement? When people offer something so valuable, immediately thank them for the act of kindness and ask if they see any other blind spots you might have. You'll be giving up any illusions of being perfect — but in reality you'll be taking a step in that direction.

72. Cull Your Professional Circle

High-altitude mountain climbers obsess over minimizing the loads they carry on their backs. They buy expensive, ultra-light, titanium cooking pots. They cut all the labels from their clothing. They chop their toothbrush in half — or leave it at home. They will do anything to increase efficiency and reduce the effect of gravity, and for good reason. The pursuit comes with a high mortality rate. Prominent alpinist Mark Twight describes the incentive structure like this: "After mediocrity comes the ground."

And so it is with you and investing.

Get better at cutting dead weight. This may mean walking away from some of your early professional acquaintances. In the beginning of your career, before you knew what you were doing, you may have built relationships with a gaggle of researchers and service providers. But because you didn't yet know what you needed, you used surrogate markers to identify people who could help you do your job. So a subset of your current relationships have only this veneer — composure, beauty, wit, age, athletic pedigree, gravitas — these are their hollow offerings. As time passes, you will realize that despite their skills, not all of these people are actually in a position to help you on your journey.

There is also another breed of acquaintance whose currency is talk. Never short of something to say, they are unburdened by the need to be correct. Just remember the old saying: opinions are like spleens— everybody has one (or something like that).

Time is scarce. During work hours, spend it with two types of people: those who can help you, and those you can help. Everyone else can wait until happy hour.

73. Choose Your Heroes Carefully...

On flights home from Las Vegas, there are always one or two passengers speaking just a little too loudly. It usually sounds something like: "I started with $500, then I was down to $50, then I put it on red 7 and..." You know the rest of the story, and so do the rest of the passengers, as the thousands of dollars of winnings are first used to fund one too many minis from the service cart. The rest of the plane, however, is usually quiet.

What do these quiet, listening, losing passengers learn? They were in the same town, at the same casinos, playing the same games. Do they count the large number of losers relative to the handful of winners? Do they notice the extraordinarily small number of big winners? Do they compare the winner's take with the cumulative losses of the unlucky ones? Or, in spite of all reason, do they learn that anyone can hit it big in Vegas?

Yes, winners are a special subset. They can always point to the scoreboard as their proof. They write history, and they exhibit Bloody Mary-fueled braggadocio on the Vegas flight.

But look closer. Not all successes are equal.

Winners are a heterogeneous bunch. Among with the small sliver who earned it are mixed in the lucky, the cheaters, the temporarily successful, and the liars. Before you celebrate them, emulate their techniques, or buy their book, take a moment to understand how they won. Many of the people who are today's investing gods are just the guy on the plane...success will visit them but will not stay.

When choosing your investing heroes, carefully discern the winners who exhibit repeatable success. At least here you can pick up techniques that could help you beat the casino tomorrow. Have a close look at the style of these specimens and borrow everything you can.

74. ...But Run Your Own Race

There are limits to the lessons you can collect by studying other successful investors. In the beginning of your career, there's a lot to be gained. But as the years pass, eventually your early apprenticeship ends. You learn less and less from each expert, until eventually you will reach a level of competence where the value of studying the latest icon is uncertain. You become like a chef who has the ingredients of a recipe, but you don't know exactly how to put them all together. You can taste the master's lemon meringue, but when you try to bake one, you just end up with sour pie.

No matter how carefully you study the lords of finance, and how completely you assimilate their methods, you cannot *become* them. You are a different vessel, and you will need to develop your own style that suits your own strengths.

From your differences can rise unique comparative advantages. Think of the parallels in the athletic realm. When Dick Fosbury first turned his back to the high-jump bar. When Muhammad Ali turned desperate defense — being pinned against the ropes — into his "rope-a-dope" weapon. When gold-medalist Michael

Johnson spurned the classic sprinter's gazelle-stride with steps so short and choppy that he looked like a sewing machine on legs.

Like these athletes, you will have to part with your mentors to go beyond them. When the starting gun goes off and your own performance begins to be measured, you will have to run your own race.

75. The Math You Learned In B-School Is Wrong

Maybe you have an MBA or have taken some introductory statistics courses. If so, you are certainly familiar with the graphical hummock known as the normal distribution, the perfectly symmetric bell curve which can be fully described by two numbers, the center of the curve (the mean) and a measure of its breadth (standard deviation.) (If you haven't been to business school, feel free to skip this chapter: you don't need to be de-programmed!)

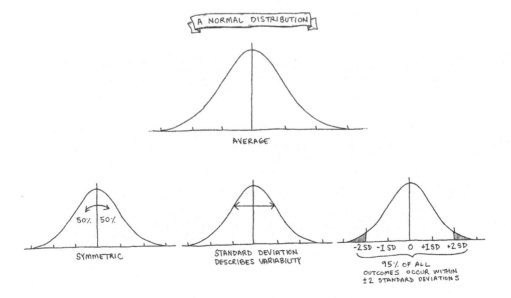

A NORMAL DISTRIBUTION

AVERAGE

SYMMETRIC

STANDARD DEVIATION DESCRIBES VARIABILITY

-2SD -1SD 0 +1SD +2SD

95% OF ALL OUTCOMES OCCUR WITHIN ±2 STANDARD DEVIATIONS

In finance, normal distributions have been adopted to describe the nature of returns of all asset classes, including stocks. In the late 1950s, Harry Markowitz pioneered modern portfolio theory, positing that risk-averse investors will combine assets in a way that maximizes returns for their chosen amount of risk.

Harry had to make some assumptions to get his theory to work, including the ideas that all investors are rational, are risk-averse, have access to the same information at the same time, and don't have to pay taxes or transaction costs. He also assumed that investors know the risk and return profile of any asset, the way that assets move relative to one another, and that these things never change. That is only a partial list, but for the moment, let's be generous and assume all of this is true.

The one additional, whopping assumption at the center of this theory is that each asset is described by the normal distribution. If you buy something, your future return will be described by this upside-down bowl. You have the highest chance of returning the exact average return, and your chances of receiving a better or worse outcome decline symmetrically as you move away from average. Eventually as you move very far from the center, your chances of getting a very large or very small payout approach zero identically.

The problem with using the normal distribution to describe the movement of stocks is that it isn't true. This model is an overgeneralized stretch...it only *resembles* how the world works. It would be as if you announced a new hypothesis that described automobile speed. In your model, average speed of all cars is 40 mph (about 65 kph). Of course this would include a few assumptions, including that cars never run out of gas, there are no traffic jams, speed limits are infinite, and weather is constant.

You could use your model to describe the likely speed of a group of cars, regardless of how old they are, how much horsepower they have, and where they are. End result: it wouldn't matter if you were looking at Mini Coopers parked at Tesco or Formula One cars in Monaco. Your model would predict an average speed of 40 mph, with an equal chance of going faster or slower.

The real world looks like this: the next speed of a parked Mini Cooper is reliably *negative*, as drivers reverse out of their parking spaces. The average speed of a lap at the Monaco Grand Prix often exceeds 100 mph (160 kph). And Harry Markowitz? When asked how he allocated his personal financial assets between stock and bonds, the father of quantitative portfolio theory replied that he should have run the calculations to determine proper weights for each, but instead he just split it 50/50.

There are four ways that Modern Portfolio Theory falls down that deserve special mention:

1) The distribution of stock returns aren't symmetric.
Market results do not follow a shapely curve, normal or otherwise. For starters, they can go up hundreds of percent, but they can only go down to zero. Also, for certain populations of stocks, the distribution of future returns can be tilted to the right (stocks trading below levels of tangible book value or net cash, stocks with high but safe dividend yields) or the left (ultra-high multiple, cash-flow-negative story stocks.)

2) The distribution isn't normally shaped.

Those dainty wings at the sides of the normal distribution indicate that extreme events are very unlikely. This doesn't remotely resemble reality — extremely good, and bad, things happen all the time. In statistic-speak, the "tails" of the distribution are fatter. This explains why value-at-risk models often fail at critical moments, and why the quants you know can sometimes be found wandering around your office explaining why their model was blown up by a rare, sixth standard deviation event. Again.

3) The average moves around.

The expected return of an asset class is not a constant, but rather moves up or down as it is formed by prior events, valuation, and external variables (think interest rates, legislative intervention, or tax policy.) Gold is a good example. After the Bretton-Woods meetings in 1949, gold prices were fixed at $35/oz. For the next 22 years. Gold's expected return was exactly 0%. Even more extreme was U.S. President Franklin Delano Roosevelt's 1933 executive order #6102, which criminalized any personal ownership of gold and generously allowed you 25 days to surrender any you owned to the government.

4) The breadth of the curve isn't fixed.

Even if a normally shaped distribution did describe the way stocks work, on different days it is a different *size* normal distribution. Size is determined by risk, and investors can often change their minds about how risky something is. (This is why the VIX index, a measure of stock market volatility, isn't a flat line.) The standard deviations of entire asset classes can change suddenly as they are buffeted by economic, legislative or geopolitical developments.

Why does any of this matter?

The investing world is not a well-organized place where pretty, symmetric curves describe reality. The real curve is skewed, discontinuous, and most importantly, unsettled. It's not a Botticelli, but rather *a movie* of different Picasso's.

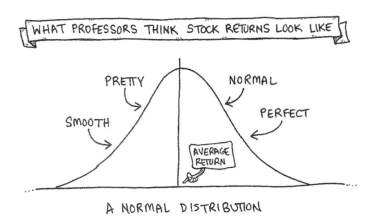

A NORMAL DISTRIBUTION

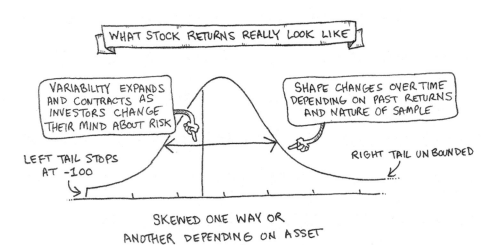

SKEWED ONE WAY OR ANOTHER DEPENDING ON ASSET CLASS

In this world, the real one, the goal is not to minimize risk. Instead, look to maximize risk on the "good," positive, right side of the range of outcomes, and minimize left-side, "bad" risk. Again, in statistic-speak, you don't want to minimize variance, but rather maximize positive semivariance (and minimize negative semivariance.) Get better at spotting those choppy, *ab*-normal distributions that are distorted in your favor.

76. The Most Productive Time

Jesse Livermore, an early 1900s trader regarded as the greatest who ever lived, believed it was important to disconnect from the tape for a restorative break. He would often walk away from the markets for months at a time. His advice: "Money is made by sitting, not trading."

Some things have changed since Livermore's day, and some haven't. The modern reality of this profession is a deluge of colliding information and responsibility. It oftentimes has all the pleasantness of being buried alive, with the redeeming feature that it is sometimes more profitable. The demands on your time far exceed available minutes, so you are constantly confronted with the challenge of prioritizing a wall of information. Filtering and ranking — simply figuring out what to do next — takes a lot of oxygen even before you begin the actual job itself. However, there is a beat in time when all of this temporarily recedes. It is the moment after you return from a vacation.

This is the transitory moment of noiseless clarity, when your professional acuity is crisper than at any other hour of your life. Because your mental bandwidth isn't being consumed with trifles, you can see things more clearly. It's like being granted a superpower — intellectual x-ray vision — for a day. Correlations, trends, patterns, truths...at this moment they will all come to you.

Vacations reboot your mind because they clear the cerebral congestion that builds over months of continuous effort. Removed from the stressors of daily life, your brain re-builds its reservoirs of motivation, attention and creativity. Your thinking unsticks from its daily pathways, and as your mind wanders you can now connect different ideas in unexpected ways.

Beware: this souvenir you have brought back — heightened perception — is perishable. The best case is that it lasts several days, but realistically it will be much shorter. Don't waste it! Emails can wait. So can absolutely every other pettiness — these things will still be there for you when you're ready. Now is the moment for strategy, conclusion, and action.

Without a short periodic rest, your professional command will suffer. Your decision-making can weaken and slow, you can become exhausted or ill, and your irritability can increase. Nobody wants to work with a dull-witted, sniffling grouch. Take a vacation every once in a while.

77. The Most Dangerous Time

The most dangerous time in investing is after you have had a big success. Your investment prowess is on display, and damn you look good!

Positive reinforcement peppers you from all directions. Your body is flush with financial endorphins, and your pockets are flush with cash. You just bought new clothes and shoes, because you deserve them, right? As you walk the office halls, everyone hails you with a high-five or a fist-bump or whatever greeting the urban professional class most recently borrowed from the Crips as they shout your name with extra letters attached (yesterday you were "Steve" but today it's "Hey Steve-O!" Susan becomes "Suz-E-Q!"). The glare is bright. You even think your dog is smiling at you.

During Roman times, when military commanders returned from successful campaigns, they were rewarded with a tumultuous ceremony called a triumph, where the citizenry would turn out to celebrate the victor. It was basically an ancient ticker tape parade combining dancing, public games, bawdy singing, and sacrifices to the gods. The returning conqueror rode through the streets of Rome in a gilded chariot pulled by four white horses, wearing a laurel crown and a gold-embroidered purple toga picta, swimming in the crowd's adulations.

But also in the chariot, standing just behind the hero, was a slave who had only one job. He whispered over and over again into the conquerer's ear, "Memento te mortalem esse," which translates as "Remember, thou art mortal."

During your moments of conspicuous success; after a bull market, when trailing returns are strong, when one of your stocks gets taken out at a high premium, if you sell a stock just before a precipitous drop, when you win the big account — remember, thou art mortal. It is normal and healthy to bask in the sun while it shines. Enjoy it! But don't let overconfidence infect the next decision that you make.

As a defensive measure, train yourself toward action during times of success. This is not our nature. In general, it is hard to summon the creativity to see a different future, but it's doubly difficult when surrounded by the distracting afterglow of a win. Simultaneously, the incentives to get the next decision right have a weaker pull. It is very, very hard to change when things are going well.

Perhaps the best example of how to do it comes from Bill Gates, primogenitor of Microsoft. On March 24th, 1999, Gates published his second book. At this moment his firm's stock price was near an all-time high after increasing 1,528% percent over the prior 5 years. Microsoft had an equity capitalization of $450 billion, and by this measure was not only the most valuable company in the world but also the most valuable public company in history. From this time forward, Bill Gates' name would be mentioned alongside Vanderbilt, Ford and Rockefeller.

At his moment of defining success, Gates wrote this: "In three years, every product my company makes will be obsolete. The only question is whether we will make them obsolete or somebody else will." Bill was in touch with his mortality.

Fill in the blank: After pride comes a _____. The next time somebody bumps your fist, pretend they punched you in the face instead. Wake up! Stay in motion! You are mortal!

78. The Most Crippling Time

The most debilitating time in your career will be when you are underperforming during a sharp down market. (A moment of "high downside capture" in consultant-speak.)

There are many reasons to try to avoid large declines in your portfolio. They damage your career trajectory, impact your compensation, and clients certainly don't like it. However, the most important reason to protect your portfolio from large declines is that they impair your ability to think. Risks loom larger, second-guessing and self doubt slow your thinking, and any distraction at all suddenly becomes important enough to postpone the unsettling moment when you have to make the next investment decision. Exceptionally poor performance is like a fungus that blooms quickly. Once it starts, it spreads.

The best way to treat this condition is to never get there in the first place. Many of the tops in the profession discuss a "margin of safety," which is a backstop which protects you from a dramatic loss in a security. Think of it like a car's airbag that prevents the worst-case scenario amidst a severe, unexpected event.

Margins of safety are easy to find and are cheaper than tranquilizers (the other common cure for acute underperformance). They are built piece-by-piece from the nature of each stock you select, and also by the trading relationship between each of these stocks. Use the financial statements to determine net-net working capital, then work your way up the stack to liquidation value, private market value, and a worst-case armageddon-raining-frogs-plague-of-locusts cash flow projection. Invest in companies where the current share price isn't much different from your calculations. Don't forget to check your portfolio for cross correlations among holdings (there are software tools for this), to confirm that you are as diversified as you would like to be.

There are old portfolio managers and there are bold portfolio managers, but there are no old, bold portfolio managers. One old portfolio manager I know talks about "winning ugly." These are the days when the market is down, but he loses less than his benchmark. His attention to the margin of safety protects him on these days. He is the most relaxed PM I have ever met.

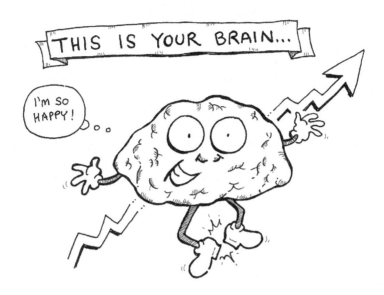

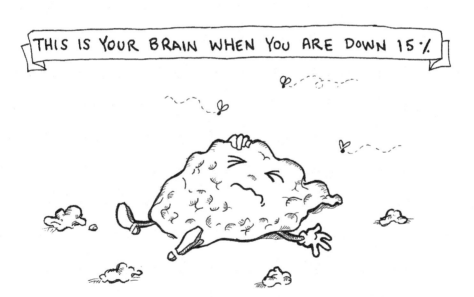

79. Do Not Invest With Cheating Bastards

Life is simply too short to invest with malfeasant company management teams. Really, why would you do it? There are plenty of companies who aren't helmed by dubious, potential psychopaths. Why not choose from those instead?

Who am I talking about? The CEO who escaped conviction on a technicality and is back at the helm. The CFO who has chosen the aggressive revenue recognition policies, where the cash flows don't match earnings. The board members who overlook self-dealing and just happen to know one another from a previous company. The COO with the resumé errors.

Ask them a hard question about any of this and they will be insulted. That's the tell. They might also frame their actions as standard industry practice, or disparage your analysis. Each of these responses, "How dare you!", "Everybody's doing it", and "You just don't get it" are juvenile non-answers. Pay attention when you hear them.

If you choose to invest with honest but simply incapable management, that is OK. There is a price for B and C grade management. The financial position and cash flows from the firm are tangible. And many businesses run well despite middling leadership.

But none of this is true with liars and thieves. With them, you need to come to terms with the following realities: what you see is not real. No matter how good it looks (and it will look and sound very good), it is an illusion. There is no balance sheet —no financial statements at all, for that matter. For these reasons, there is also no margin of safety and thus no backstop. These set-ups are mousetraps, and you are the mouse.

80. Do Something

I once met a firm's Chairman of the Board who was an old Australian Brigadier General. He was right out of central casting: Ruler-straight back, swoop of silver hair, piercing O'Toole-blue eyes, gravelly voice. He told me a story, in the intoxicating way that only old warriors can, about his first command. It was World War II. Europe. The week before he had advanced in rank when his superior officer was shot by a sniper. He was 19-years-old.

Now he and his men were being shelled, and in the horrific chaos with injuries and casualties mounting, he radioed up the chain of command and asked what he should do. Thus came the reply: "Bloody hell do *something!*"

That was it.

Your journey through the land of portfolio management will not be all champagne and sunshine. Some extremely uncomfortable moments await. When times are bad and you look across your portfolio battlefield and see casualties mounting, do something!

Diagnose. Trim, add, or sell. Confirm your hypothesis or rotate to a new one. Discuss with others whom you respect. Explore a new industry. Re-center on your comparative advantage. Use different tools. Redeploy. Move!

81. The Earth Is Not The Center Of The Universe

Ideas about how the world works change slowly. Perhaps the best example is Galileo, who in 1626 published *Dialogue Concerning The Two Chief World Systems.* The book resurrected Copernicus's theory of heliocentricity — the idea that the sun is the center of our system and that the earth and planets revolve around it.

Of course, this wasn't copacetic with the Church, which insisted that God himself placed Earth and man properly at the center of the universe. Pope Urban VIII called Galileo to Rome, where he was tried, found guilty of heresy, and excommunicated. Prisoner rights and GPS ankle bracelets hadn't been invented yet, and so the standard punishment for heresy was to be burned at the stake. Galileo escaped this fate only by recanting his position, but he spent the rest of his life under house arrest, until his death in 1642.

For hundreds of years, the leading universities of Europe continued to teach that the earth was the center of the universe. It wasn't until 1992, 350 years after Galileo's death, that Pope John Paul II finally lifted his excommunication. Ideas die hard.

The investing world, too, has its share of deeply entrenched beliefs. Similar to geocentricity, they are long held and hard to change. To suggest anything else is heresy, and yet some of them are wrong. We have some ideas about risk and return, for example, that are looking a little geocentric. Every finance textbook, every 401(k) website, every broker's slide deck has a chart that looks like this:

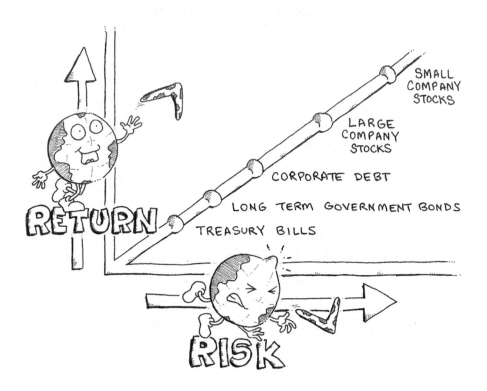

This is the finance industry's current cosmology. The world is two dimensional (risk vs. return), equities are riskier than bonds, and both risk and return increase as company size decreases. Greater than 95% of investors believe all of this to be true. They are wrong.

First, in the stock market, you do not have to take more risk to achieve more return. Heresy, you say? Look at the data for value stocks compared to growth stocks below.

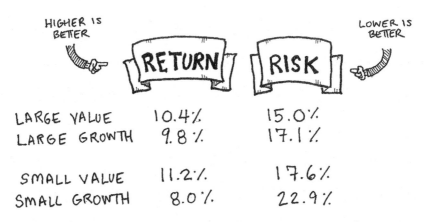

	RETURN	RISK
	HIGHER IS BETTER	LOWER IS BETTER
LARGE VALUE	10.4%	15.0%
LARGE GROWTH	9.8%	17.1%
SMALL VALUE	11.2%	17.6%
SMALL GROWTH	8.0%	22.9%

(ANNUALIZED RETURN AND STANDARD DEVIATION, 1985-2013)

("LARGE" = RUSSELL TOP 200, "SMALL" = RUSSELL 2000; SOURCE: MORNINGSTAR)

Geocentric finance is flawed. The reality is that value investing offers not only less risk but more return. This truth doesn't fit neatly onto the diagonal risk/return line, but it is the truth nonetheless.

Another bedrock, conventional belief depicted on this chart: stocks are riskier than bonds. This adequately describes most observations, just like the sun rotating around a fixed earth could describe the appearance of day and night. But it's not that simple.

Bonds have been on a 20-year run. Today, interest rates are near zero, and governments around the world have been unanimously printing currency to service existing debt. Are you certain those bonds are safe? Sure, nominally you are seeing less volatility. But what about the purchasing power of the yield stream?

In contrast, equities are adaptive — management can do a lot of things to fight input inflation: raise prices, increase efficiencies, enter new markets. Bonds not so much; there's a reason it's called *fixed* income. Are bonds less risky then stocks? The truth is, it depends...

All of us have a collection of beliefs which we use to make decisions in a complex world. We need these intellectual shortcuts or we would never get anything done. When it comes to asset allocation, however, there are some gaping differences between how we think the world works and reality. Be careful what you believe.

82. What To Listen To

Need a soundtrack for your investing? These songs are guaranteed*
to improve your investment returns!

"Mo Money, Mo Problems," Notorious B.I.G.
"Everything Counts," Depeche Mode
"For the Love of Money," The O'Jays
"Free Money," Patti Smith
"With Plenty of Money and You," Count Basie and Tony Bennett
"I Need a Dollar," Aloe Blacc
"If You've Got the Money, I've Got the Time," Willie Nelson
"Opportunities (Let's Make Lots of Money)," The Pet Shop Boys
"Money Talks," Rick James
"Ka Ching!," Shania Twain
"Take the Money and Run," The Steve Miller Band
"Independent Women," Destiny's Child
"Money," Pink Floyd
"Money," The Flying Lizards
"Money, Money," Grateful Dead
"Money, Money," Liza Minelli
"Money, Money, Money," Abba
"Gold Digger," Kanye West and Jamie Foxx

"Money Machine," James Taylor

"Just Got Paid," N'Sync

"I Want Your Love," Transvision Vamp

"Love Money Can't Buy," John Lee Hooker

"Rich Girl," Daryl Hall and John Oates

"If I Had $1,000,000," Barenaked Ladies

"Dime, Quarter, Nickel, Penny," Nappy Roots

"The Money Song," Dean Martin and Jerry Lewis

"C.R.E.A.M.," Wu-Tang Clan

"The Gambler," Kenny Rogers

"Money Made," AC/DC

"Price Tag," Jessie J. Featuring B.o.B

"Greenbacks," Ray Charles

"Money Bought," Nickelback

"It's Money That I Love," Randy Newman

"Takin' Care of Business," Bachman Turner Overdrive

"The L&N Don't Stop Here Anymore," Michelle Shocked

"Gimme Some Money," Spinal Tap

"Cash, Money, Cars, Clothes," Ruff Endz

"How to be a Millionaire," ABC

"Hold to Your Money," Howlin Wolf

"Between Angels and Insects," Papa Roach

"Brother Can You Spare a Dime," Bing Crosby

(*not really)

83. Into Every Portfolio A Little Rain Must Fall

Don't learn too much from your mistakes. When one of the original founding partners retired from my firm, the reason he gave was, "This is a young man's game." He was 53. I don't know, maybe he was having trouble mustering the strength to bang the keyboard on his Bloomberg terminal, which he did every time the wrong headline scrolled by. But more likely, after years of experience, he had intellectually painted himself into a corner and was having trouble making the next decision. It's not really that it's a young man's (or woman's) game, but it certainly is a game for people who can forgive themselves.

There are people like this in every office. They are the seasoned old guard, quick with the math, who have seemingly bottomless company-specific knowledge and are sure about their conclusions. The problem is, the conclusion has become almost always the same: No. They will give you three... no four... no *five* reasons why the stock you just pitched is a bad idea. Every new potential investment recalls a catalog of memories — risks, similar to the one you're contemplating, gone wrong.

So as you go through your career, be very careful about what you learn from your losses. There are lessons to be learned in the investing graveyard, but there are some risks taken that — given similar circumstances — you should probably take again.

84. Go With The Flow

Free cash flow is an umbrella that protects, an elixir that heals, and a fuel that powers companies. It is a financial wonder drug.

Seek firms that generate it.

By free cash flow, I mean the cash generated by a firm after all its operating needs are paid for. Generally it is calculated by taking the net income of a firm, adding back non-cash charges like depreciation and amortization, and subtracting capital expenditures required to sustain the business. You can think of it as a way of removing the distortions of accrual accounting and revealing the cash profits of a firm.

Companies that generate free cash flow don't go bankrupt. In fact, as time passes, these firms increase in value. And as the cliché goes, "you get paid to wait." This value can come to you in a few ways: via organic expansion, dividend, share repurchase, or growth of that first and most beautiful line on the balance sheet, "Cash."

Some out-of-favor companies, even in their darkest moment, can generate cash. With these turnaround situations the clock doesn't tick as fast. Management has time to plan with a longer, strategic horizon rather than the garage sale tactics of cash-flow-negative firms that are forced to hurriedly trade their most valuable assets. (These firms are left like a hockey player on the ice who just sold his skates. The end comes quickly.)

In addition to having more time, companies that produce cash are generating the very raw material that will be needed to dig themselves out of the hole. So they are, at least to a degree, self-funding, which is a great thing to be during moments when investors are less enamored with your business.

85. You Are Not Baking Cookies

Recipes for investment success are not dependable. Although there are bedrock truths in investing, how you source, mix, and weight these ingredients can change. Some of these shifts are subtle, temporary, and probably best ignored. Others are tectonic.

Recently I gave a speech to a graduate business school audience about portfolio management and risk-control techniques. Although at the MBA level you can never be sure if the audience is there for the wisdom, the potential internship, or the free pizza, this group seemed engaged. The event was going smoothly until I opened up the floor for questions. First question: "What about SRI (Socially Responsible Investing)?" Umm... Second question: "Do you use ESG (Environmental, Social and Governance) scores in your allocation decisions?" Huh? Weren't these supposed to be the bloodless young capitalists who would eat their own young for a dollar?

No, these were millennials. I mumbled something about good ethics being good business, and pointed out that there was more pizza left if anyone was hungry.

At that moment I was reminded that the rules are continually changing. In 10 years these students will be piloting large pools of capital, driving stocks in one direction or another, and when they do, SRI, ESG, and whatever acronym comes next will have an influence on share prices.

One of the unfortunate realities of this undertaking is that both art and science evolve and shift with the passage of time. Some of this is technological, such as the evolution from boys in alpaca jackets writing quotes on a chalkboard (alpaca wool didn't smear the chalk), to ticker tapes, to private fiber-optic cables pumping high-frequency quotes.

Other changes are caused by alterations in market structure as broad swaths of stocks are torqued by changes in tax policy, legal or regulatory backdrop, informational accessibility, or liquidity. Dividend-paying stocks and the tobacco industry, for example, are two classes of equity that are perceived very differently today than, say, 1995. Here the rules have changed, literally.

In the mid 90s, a very capable analyst at my shop was anchored to the hypothesis "No lawsuit has ever been successful against big tobacco." This was a reasonable and even common position at the time. After all, it had been true for decades, until suddenly one Friday afternoon in 1996, it wasn't. The dislocation in Philip Morris, one of the largest, most liquid Dow components, was so great that trading had to be halted. This was a problem because we owned it in every single client account. When the stock finally reopened the following Monday, the size and volume of the share price decline made Niagara Falls look like a garden hose. The world had suddenly changed. Eventually, it cost the analyst his job.

Still other changes come as we better understand human nature. How we value success and fear failure. How allocation decisions are born within us. How demographic changes interact with capital allocation.

It seems that we are not sterile, static rational maximizers after all, and that some of the central assumptions of economics, in certain situations, are in play. Jut ask those MBAs.

It's important to remain consistent as you deploy your comparative advantage in the markets, whatever it may be. To "stick to your knitting" as they say. However, stay alert. You are not baking cookies. The tools for getting the job done, plus the quality of the ingredients and even the recipe itself, can change.

86. You Are In Viking Heaven

In Norse legend, after death in combat, the best warriors were hand-picked by Odin and led to Valhalla, "the hall of the slain," by the beautiful Valkyries. Valhalla was a vast hall with 540 doors, wide enough for 800 warriors standing shoulder to shoulder to pass through. Spears formed the rafters, and the roof was thatched with shields and breastplates. In Valhalla, the warriors spent their time preparing for the Ragnarök, the final battle with the gods on the battlefield Vígríðr.

They did this by fighting all day and partying all night. Each day the Einherjar, as the warriors of Valhalla were called, tuned their speed, strength, and battle skills in blood-soaked, often fatal combat. At night, they gorged on the meat of Sæhrímnir, the great boar, as the Valkyries served them mead and other delights.

The warrior Einherjar also enjoyed one incredibly special bonus. At least until the Ragnarök happened, they were immortal. Each night, after Sæhrímnir the boar was consumed, it was resurrected to provide sustenance for the next day. The Valkyries returned each night as virgins. And for Valhalla's fighters, it was the same, as even the mortally wounded were brought back to life to feast and drink with their comrades so they could be ready again for the next day's battle. Every day was a new day.

The stock market is financial Valhalla. Each day can be a battle. You can enjoy euphoric victory or suffer humiliating, dispiriting defeat. But even if you were slain yesterday, today you can rise again, ready to join a new fight. Wiser. Faster. Stronger. Every day offers fresh combat with new information, prices and news.

For many among us — and maybe you are one of them — until our own personal final meeting with the gods comes, it is heaven.

Acknowledgments

First, to the old crew at Tobey Village, who taught me most of what is here, and whose ideas I have borrowed shamelessly. Thank you all for providing exactly the right mix of opportunity, encouragement, and criticism during the journey. Of course special thanks to Mike and Geoff for making it all happen in the first place.

Thank you to all of the wonderful people at Federated Investors for your companionship, support, and the opportunity to serve.

Many thanks to my friends at other firms in the asset management industry. I am humbled and blessed to be among you. I have enjoyed every minute of our conversations, and am already looking forward to our next chat.

Thanks to all who helped with the production of this book in one way or another. Especially to those who gave constructive feedback along the way: Annie, Paul, Jeff, Joan, Brian, Pam, Dave, John, Mark, Matt, Gregg, Bill, Dan and of course my editor, Mark Liu. The climb is always harder closer to the summit...and you helped me get all the way on this one. I will be forever grateful.

Lastly, and most importantly, to my wife, children, and parents — thank you for being my bedrock foundation, my anchor to windward, and my north star.

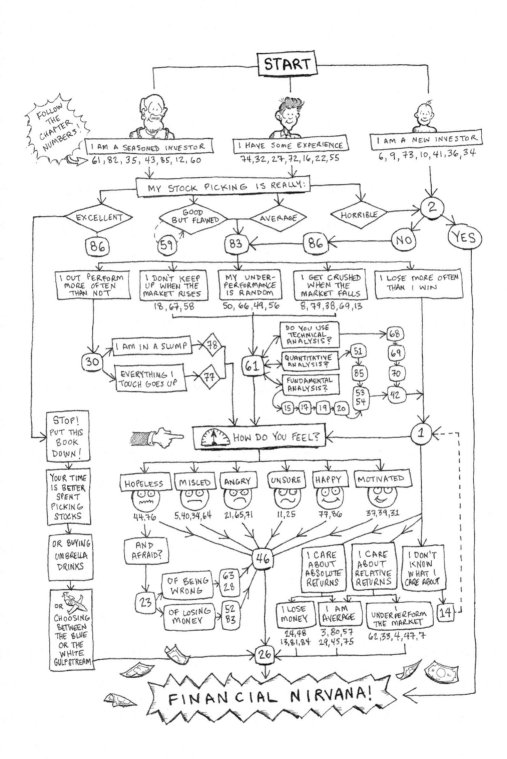

About the Author

Lawrence Creatura has been in the asset management industry for more than 20 years. He has invested long and short, conducted research in every economic sector, run funds of every stripe... and has the scars to show for it. He is excited to share some of the "Road Rules" of investing in *Long and Short: Confessions of a Portfolio Manager.*

Lawrence has appeared on CNBC, Bloomberg, and The Street, and has been quoted in the Wall Street Journal, Barron's, The Financial Times, The New York Times, MarketWatch, The Washington Post, USA Today, CNNMoney, The San Jose Mercury News, CBS News, The Los Angeles Times, Wall Street Daily, The Boston Globe, Crain's New York Business, The Dallas Morning News, The Wall Street Transcript, The Seattle Times, U.S. News and World Report, Businessweek, The Chicago Tribune, and Investor's Business Daily.

In his spare time, Lawrence is an amateur mountain climber, having completed ascents in Alaska, Nepal, Irian Jaya, Western Canada, Bolivia, Patagonia and Kazakhstan.

He lives in Upstate N.Y. with his wife and four children.

CPSIA information can be obtained at www.ICGtesting.com
Printed in the USA
BVOW06*0603060416

443162BV00008B/143/P